MW01201295

Asteroids in Astrology 4

Outer Main Belt Asteroids: Trojans, Hilda, Cybele
Series: Asteroids in Astrology 4
Author: Benjamin Adamah

Lay-out: Sylvia Carrilho

ISBN 978-94-92355-69-0

Publisher:

VAMzzz Publishing
P.O. Box 3340
1001 AC Amsterdam
The Netherlands
www.vamzzz.com
vamzzz@protonmail.com

ASTEROIDS IN ASTROLOGY 4

Outer Main Belt Asteroids:
TROJANS HILDA CYBELE

Benjamin Adamah

VAMzzz PUBLISHING

CONTENTS

6

INTRODUCTION

BEYOND THE MAIN BELT

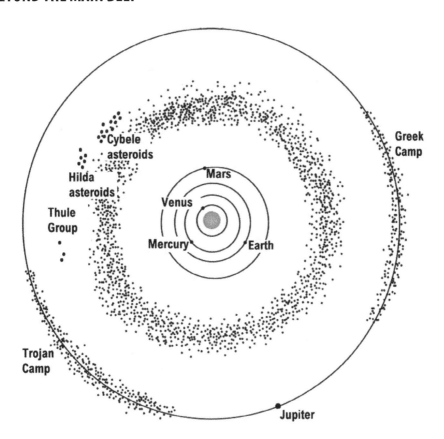

The first three parts of this series on asteroid astrology, in addition to Centaurs and ex-Comets, primarily describe distant to very distant objects such as Plutinos, Cubewanos, Haumeans, Scattered Disc Objects, Sedna, and various TNOs with deviant Neptune resonances.

Part four is the first volume focusing on the more classical asteroids, many of which were discovered in the 19th and early 20th centuries. Astrologically, asteroids cannot be rigidly assigned to a specific asteroid group.

Nevertheless, in some groups such as the Plutinos or the Centaurs, strong group characteristics emerge, bringing us a bit closer to understanding the solar system and our interaction with it. Particularly interesting are possible correlations between astronomical positions and qualities (e.g., asteroid composition or resonant alignment with a planet) and their translation into astrological significance.

TROJANS AND JUPITER TROJANS

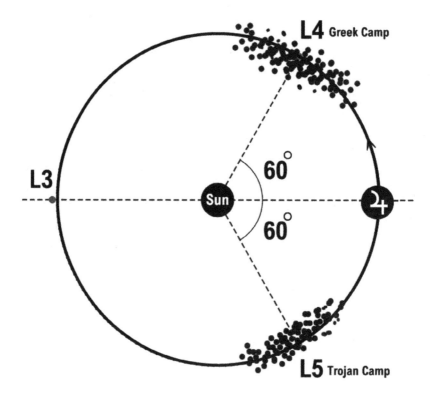

Trojans are fascinating objects in this regard. Jupiter Trojans are widely known, but there are also Earth, Venus, Mars, Saturn-Moon, Uranus, and Neptune Trojans. Since Trojans share the same orbit as the planets they are linked to, a certain consistency can be expected within the nuances of their astrological interpretations.

With Jupiter Trojans, this often manifests as an overload of Yang energy, leading to various challenges and attempts to find stability.

Trojans in astronomy refer to small celestial bodies, predominantly asteroids, sharing the orbit of a larger celestial body and maintaining a stable position approximately 60° ahead of or behind the main body near Lagrangian points L4 and L5. These Lagrangian points represent areas where gravitational forces allow for a delicate balance between the primary celestial body, such as a star or a planet, and a much smaller object located at one of these Lagrangian points.

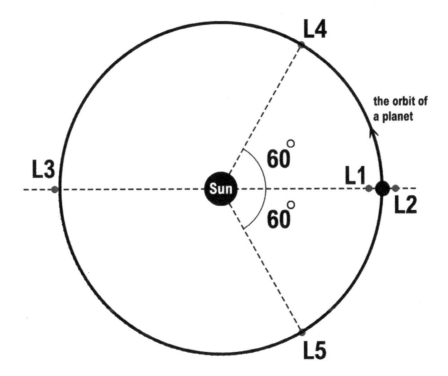

In the Solar System, most Trojans are associated with Jupiter, forming the Greek camp at L4 (ahead of Jupiter) and the Trojan camp at L5 (trailing Jupiter). Over a million Jupiter Trojans larger than one kilometer are estimated to exist, with more than 7,000 currently catalogued. Other Trojans include those associated with Mars, Neptune, Uranus, and Earth, with only nine Mars Trojans, 28 Neptune Trojans, two Uranus Trojans, and two Earth Trojans identified to date. There is also a temporary Venus-trojan.

The term 'trojan' originated with the discovery of 'trojan asteroids' near Jupiter's Lagrangian points. These asteroids are named after figures from the Trojan War of Greek mythology, following a convention where those near L4 are named for Greek characters, and those near L5 are named for Trojan characters. There are two exceptions, which were named before the convention was put in place, 624 Hector (Trojan hero) located at the L4 point, and 617 Patroclus (Greek hero) at the L5 point. The Jovian Trojans are estimated to be as numerous as asteroids in the asteroid belt.

Trojans have been found near the Lagrangian points of other planets, including Neptune, Mars, Earth, Uranus, and Venus. Minor planets near these Lagrangian points may be referred to as Lagrangian minor planets. There are 28 known Neptunian Trojans, with the expectation that large Neptunian Trojans outnumber large Jovian Trojans by an order of magnitude.

Specific Trojans include 2010 TK7, the first known Earth trojan, confirmed in 2011, and 2020 XL5, identified in 2021. Uranus has its first trojan, 2011 QF99, located at the L4 Lagrangian point, with a second one, 2014 YX49, announced in 2017. Additionally, 2013 ND15 is a temporary Venusian-trojan. Even the large asteroids Ceres and Vesta host temporary Trojans in their orbits.

This book predominantly features descriptions of Jupiter Trojans. However, I have also covered some Mars Trojans, the only Uranus Trojan with an MPC number, several Neptune Trojans, and two deviant yet remarkable and astrologically interesting objects.

CLASSIC TROJANS, CO-ORBITAL ASTEROIDS AND QUASI-SATELLITES

Apart from Trojans I have also described the astrological meaning of some related bodies: co-orbital asteroids, and quasi-satellites. The astronomical differences between classic Trojans, co-orbital asteroids, and quasi-satellites primarily involve their orbital configurations and relationships with larger celestial bodies.

Classic Trojan Asteroids
Orbit: Classic Trojans are located at stable Lagrange points, specifically the L4 and L5 points, which are 60 degrees ahead of and behind a larger planet in its orbit, respectively.
Stability: They remain in these Lagrange points due to gravitational equilibrium with the larger planet.

Co-orbital Asteroids
Orbit: Co-orbital asteroids share a similar or nearly identical orbit with a larger

celestial body but do not necessarily occupy stable Lagrange points.
Stability: Their orbits may be influenced by gravitational perturbations, leading
to variations over time.

Quasi-satellites
Orbit: Quasi-satellites are objects that orbit the Sun but, from the perspective
of an observer on the larger celestial body, appear to have an oscillating,
horseshoe-shaped orbit around it.
Stability: They are not true satellites and are not in stable orbits around the
larger body. Instead, they have a complex, quasi-periodic motion.

In summary, classic Trojan asteroids are stable at Lagrange points, co-orbital
asteroids share orbits without being in Lagrange points, and quasi-satellites
have orbits that give the appearance of oscillation around a larger body
but lack stability as true satellites. These distinctions arise from the specific
gravitational dynamics and interactions in their orbital configurations.

HILDA ASTEROIDS

*Many Hilda-asteroids, including the subgroup of Schubart-asteroids, can be
highly intense with a tendency toward somewhat Plutonian compulsion.*

The Hilda asteroids, over 5,000 in number, constitute a distinctive dynamical
group situated beyond the asteroid belt within Jupiter's orbit, maintaining a
3:2 orbital resonance with Jupiter. Discovered by German astronomer Max
Wolf on August 17, 1928, 153 Hilda serves as the group's namesake. Their
elliptical orbits strategically align with Jupiter's Lagrange points, ensuring
synchronization with the L5, L4, or L3 points in each successive orbit.
Characterized by a semi-major axis between 3.7 and 4.2 AU, eccentricity
below 0.3, and inclination under 20°, the Hilda asteroids form two collisional
families: the Hilda family and the Schubart family, named after 1911 Schubart.
Predominantly displaying low-albedo D-type and P-type surface colors, some
are of C-type.

The Hildas, in 3:2 resonance with Jupiter, trace a dynamic triangular figure,
the 'Hildas Triangle', maintaining stability over time. Noteworthy is their
retrograde perihelion motion, with variable orbital elements preventing
destabilization during close encounters with Jupiter. Quasi-periodical waves
in their density, greater at apexes than within the sides, reflect the Hildas'

synchronized motion. Their intersection with Trojans, varying dispersion velocities, and need for continued observations to understand their peculiarities emphasize the complexity of Hilda asteroids in our solar system.

The Schubart asteroids are considered a subcategory of the Hildas due to their shared dynamical characteristics and orbital resonance with Jupiter. The Hildas, as a group of asteroids, are defined by their 3:2 mean-motion resonance with Jupiter, meaning they complete approximately two-thirds of an orbit around the Sun for every one orbit of Jupiter. This resonance keeps them in a stable configuration relative to Jupiter's gravitational influence.

The Schubart family, named after the asteroid 1911 Schubart, is a specific cluster within the broader Hilda group. This family likely originated from a common ancestor that underwent a collisional breakup, resulting in a group of asteroids with similar orbital properties. The identification of such families helps astronomers understand the dynamical evolution and history of asteroid populations in the solar system.

In summary, the Schubart asteroids are a subset of the Hildas, sharing the overall orbital resonance characteristics with Jupiter that define the Hilda group. Some astronomers believe the Hilda-asteroids originated in the Kuiper-belt.

CYBELE ASTEROIDS

Many Cybele asteroids also comprise dark carbon-rich material and exhibit intensity, with a notable focus on themes related to sexuality or erotic seduction.

The Cybele asteroids, also known as the 'Cybeles', form a distinctive dynamical group named after the asteroid 65 Cybele. Comprising 2034 members and several collisional families, the Cybeles are situated in a 7:4 orbital resonance with Jupiter. Their orbit is characterized by an osculating semi-major axis ranging from 3.27 to 3.70 AU, exhibiting an eccentricity below 0.3 and an inclination of less than 30°. Positioned adjacent to the outermost asteroid belt beyond the Hecuba gap, which is the 2:1 resonant zone with Jupiter, and within the region of the Hilda asteroids (3:2 resonance), the Cybeles are located before the Jupiter Trojans (1:1 resonance) farther out.

The Cybele group encompasses three recognized asteroid families: the Sylvia family (603 asteroids), the Huberta family (with the asteroids Huberta,

Hermione, Lidov and James Bradley) and the Ulla family (903 asteroids).
A potential fourth family includes a small cluster with the parent body (45657)
2000 EK. Additionally, a fifth family, named after 522 Helga, was identified in
2015.

Notable members of the Cybele asteroids include 87 Sylvia and 107 Camilla,
both triple systems with multiple satellites. Other large members comprise
121 Hermione, 76 Freia, 790 Pretoria, and 566 Stereoskopia. Believed to have
originated from the fragmentation of a larger object in the distant past, the
Cybele group predominantly consists of C- and X-type asteroids. However,
NASA's Wide-field Infrared Survey Explorer has detected albedos in some
Cybele asteroids that are characteristic of stony S-type asteroids.

THULE-ASTEROIDS

The Thule group, so far consisting of three members, is fully described in
this book. In terms of orbital periods, Cybele asteroids are around 6.5 years,
Hildas just under 8 years, and Thule asteroids have an orbital period of just
under 9 years. Jupiter Trojans, like Jupiter itself, have orbital periods of around
12 years. This implies that the impact during transits, for example, is more
significant than that of asteroids in the Main Belt with average orbital periods
ranging from 4.5 to 3.5 years.

With only 3 members so far the Thule-group is too small to say something
definite about their characteristics. However they all in their own way appear
to have a link with the perspective of the outsider, the unofficial but intriging,
the lateral perspective. They are literally outside the mainstream (Main-belt)...

TROJANS

JUPITER TROJANS

2594 ACAMAS

Strength, resilience, recuperative ability both physically and mentally; strong sex drive, where sex is often disconnected from the intimate and emotional aspects

L5-Trojan, discovered on October 4, 1978, by Charles Kowal. Acamas is the Latin form of Akamas *(tireless, relentlessly enthusiastic, vital, energetic)*. The designation indicates great endurance (especially with Mars) and an intelligent awareness or intuitive application of the interaction and synergy between, what Taoists call the 'three flowers': *enthusiasm, or spiritual* energy (shen-qi), *vital energy* (qi), and *essential life energy* (jing-qi). Acamas is additionally a sexual Trojan in which sex is often practiced or used to immediately act out an acute need for it. Acamas tends not toward spirited sex where love and sex merge, but toward secular sexual encounters. An excellent Trojan if properly aspected in the horoscope of qi-gong masters, athletes, coaches. Acamas needs only to maintain his own vitality routines disciplined, and all will be well.

The resilience to climb back up to youthful vitality even from deep valleys is remarkable in Acamas. In childhood and youth, Acamas can impart an ausdauer or strength that seems superhuman. In later life, self-aggrandizement is out of the question. Yet even in the second half of life, Acamas continues to bestow his resilience. Bruce Lee, who even recovered from a broken back and paralysis, had Acamas conjunct the Plutino 2003 VS2 *(going one's own way)*; square Moon; trine Orcus/Rhadamantus; sextile Machiavelli *(power)* and opposition Ladoga *(many false friends)*, among others. Jesse Owens had Acamas conjunct 2000 OO67/Psyche; square Moon; trine Heracles *(great power achievements)*; square Chaos. The Acamas/Psyche conjunction is striking given that he was facing massive psychic pressure from the Nazis before his super performance. Forensically, Acamas involves destructive science and science in the service of evil, among other things.

The orbital time is 11 years and 178 days.

588 ACHILLES

Transforming reaction into creation; the vulnerable spot (Achilles' heel); pain issues; converting destructive energy into constructive leads to financial progress

L4 Trojan of 135.47 km, discovered on February 22, 1906, by Max Wolf. Achilles comes from *Akhos Loas* (pain of the people), and indeed, Achilles primarily revolves around pain. Both causing pain and catalyzing or transporting it as a 'pain medium'. This Trojan has an unstable, predominantly intense energy that oscillates between vulnerability and aggression, leadership and lack of self-control, outbursts, and long-standing internalization. Because the discovery Sun is conjunct Hidalgo in Pisces, Achilles has a fragmented 'self' or core. Additionally, the conjunction of Mercury/Venus/Saturn indicates a tendency toward isolation and taking life too seriously. At the time of discovery, Achilles itself was in Leo opposite the tough Centaur Amycus. A positive Achilles can, after prolonged contemplation, suddenly explode like a bomb or rise like a star, which can be very satisfying for writers, artists, etc.

Achilles needs to learn to turn reactions to external stimuli into a source for creative expression instead of reacting defensively or internalizing these stimuli. Replacing reacting with creating, with integrity and authenticity, is the process of maturing for this Trojan. The position of Achilles in the horoscope is often a point where this needle gets stuck. With a dominant Achilles, it is crucial to sublimate the tendency to react harshly or take action into energy that is used constructively. Also, because success or failure, especially financially, depends entirely on it. What it depends on is indicated by the degree, sign, house, and aspecting. For artists with a strong Achilles, working with hard materials such as stone, concrete, iron, wood, etc., is most suitable.

The orbital period is 11 years and 307 days.

85030 ADMETOS

Untamable; highly determined; direct; hyper-aware of (modified) reality and one's own position as an individual; Luciferian; a tendency to cut off relationships; an exaggerated to unbearable emphasis on the integrity of the (sexual) partner or one's own passion; embedding oneself in a growing network of relationships, advancing in a Multi-Level Marketing system

L4 Trojan, discovered on September 24, 1960, by Cornelis Johannes van Houten, Ingrid van Houten-Groeneveld, and Tom Gehrels. Admetos is associated by various astrologers with 'the small', limitation, shrinking, or restriction. However, I can only place this in relation to a great overpowering force, where Admetos tends to position itself directly as an opponent. The name comes from the Greek *Ádmetos*, meaning *untamable* or *untamed*. And indeed, Admetos bows to no one!

My observations indicate that a strongly aspected Admetos gives tremendous fighting endurance, great strength, an inflexible will, and the potential to become such a formidable opponent that the opposing party avoids open confrontation and resorts to covert and cowardly methods. Admetos needs to learn to control its strength in the sense that it shouldn't let its integrity be flattened. Instead of engaging in direct confrontation, it should develop a smart gentleman's strategy and corresponding tactics. If this is not achieved, it comes at the expense of loved ones, especially the life partner. In the fight for justice or righteousness, Admetos can exhibit an intensity that can be sustained for an inhumanly long time, causing an average partner to be unable to endure it. Subsequently, Admetos may accuse the partner of cowardice or lack of integrity.

Obsession is a significant risk with this Trojan, and insight often comes too late. This is particularly the case in Fire signs where Admetos operates at the highest gear. If the energy can be harnessed and directed well, this Trojan can break iron with hands and tap into a great liberating creativity and power source, with more effective results than spontaneous discharge of frustrations. With an intensified Admetos, it is essential to pay attention to energy pathways, as there is a risk of a yang overload in later life, leading to undernourished yin meridians (especially with anger, the liver depletes the stomach, spleen, and large intestine meridians), which can result in breathing and heart problems. A prolonged Admetos struggle or deadlock also affects the nervous system, which is already overloaded and hyperactive with Admetos apriori. Qi-gong is highly recommended.

Dutch journalist Willem Oltmans, who was obstructed throughout his life by the Dutch state and royalty, financially kept small, and stigmatized as persona non-grata, eventually received a 6 million compensation from the state. He had an almost minute-exact opposition of Admetos - Saturn *(established order)*. Despite government harassment causing chronic health issues, he never gave up, and although he turned people against him with his often aggressive emotional expressions, friends and foes respected his impeccable honesty. Former marine, professional wrestler, now politician and whistleblower, Jesse Ventura, has Admetos conjunct 1994 GV9/Rhea/Hypnos *(extreme attention to detail for what*

happens to the Earth and awakening people from their slumber); square Sedna/
Spartacus/MANIAC *(calling underdogs to revolt)*; square Hidalgo *(putting things
in jeopardy)*; sextile the Plutino 2003 AZ84 *(extensive research)*; trine Juno *(mass
power)* and opposition 1998 WA31 *(lust for power, manipulation)*. The murdered
Dutch politician Pim Fortuyn, the greatest threat ever to the Dutch state and
royalty, had Admetos conjunct Pallas and Kaali *(radical end to prevailing politics)*
and square Uranus/Sado. Fortuyn was also a republican and advocated for the
abolition of the monarchy. He was almost certainly assassinated by a state-hired
sniper, with his official (only) murderer Folkert van der Graaf acting as a sort of
Manchurian candidate and backup bullet.

The orbital period is 12 years and 138 days.

911 AGAMEMNON

Emotional paralysis; fear of the outside world and a defensive outward demeanor; getting stuck in
a growth and development system that no longer serves you while simultanously being chronically
pressured to let go of this system and embrace something new; self-isolation; clouds of steam

L4 Trojan with a diameter of 166.66 km, discovered on March 19, 1919, by
Karl Wilhelm Reinmuth. The interpretation seems similar to that of Hector,
but while Hector tends to miss the reality check, Agamemnon revolves around
emotional contact. *Agamemnonas* literally means *very steadfast*.

Agamemnon, as an archetype, resembles the King of Pentacles in Tarot,
clinging to material power while simultaneously being in a chronic state of
fear. Here, the fear is directed towards the outside world or stepping out and
the feeling of having to fight or withstand that external world (discovery Sun
conjunct Apophis/Eris/Ceto). Agamemnon manifests a apparent certainty and
solidity that, in reality, is emotional suppression, rooted in deep-seated fear or
guilt. Agamemnon contaminates the degree position and aspecting with other
planets and bodies. Whether it's a conjunction, trine, square, or opposition,
what Agamemnon touches seems somehow unattainable or freezes.

Translated into behavioral terms, Agamemnon can react dismissively, bluntly,
or aggressively. At the same time, others see the tragedy in this, but also
the immovability. In short, this Trojan needs the necessary assistance from
defrosters, bodies that – not in aspect with Agememnon – provide enough
counterbalance. If not, someone with a strong Agamemnon might, at best,
stumble on the tragedy of the solid, hardworking boss or head of the family,

abandoned by those he loves because they can no longer tolerate his emotional unavailability, i.e., deep fear of intimacy and disclosure. In the worst case, Agamemnon may contribute substantially to violence or suicide, but generally, much more is needed than an afflicted Trojan. Everyone has Agamemnon somewhere in the horoscope and a point where emotional connection cannot be made, and there are enough situations and professions where entering emotional connections is not always advisable (surgeon, dentist, etc.).

Agamemnon was discovered in the 30th degree of Leo, conjunct Quaoar, opposite Uranus in the 30th degree of Aquarius. The energy in a dominant Agamemnon is thus stuck in a growth and development system that no longer serves, and is chronically under pressure to permanently let go of this system and embrace something new that offers more freedom. During this phase in this tension, there is a tendency to increasingly isolate oneself from anyone who does not share the self-made idealism or vice versa, isolate those with different beliefs.

Negatively, an afflicted Agamemnon can manifest as infertility, while a well-aspected Agamemnon may indicate the opposite and many children. Forensically, Agamemnon indicates clouds of steam.

The orbital period is 12 years and 18 days.

1404 AJAX

Not being duly rewarded for significant effort, struggle, or the display of great courage; setbacks; something one desires deeply but falls just short; unexpectedly having to make last-minute adjustments; learning to do something without expecting anything in return but for the sake of doing it well oneself

L4 Trojan with a diameter of 81.7 km, discovered by Karl Wilhelm Reinmuth on August 17, 1936. Ajax is named after the eponymous Greek hero from the Trojan War who took his own life due to his disappointment that someone else (usually Odysseus in most versions) received the armor of the deceased Achilles. Ajax was called the 'Shield Wall of the Greeks' because, immediately after Achilles, he was the greatest and most formidable warrior. He believed he was not fairly rewarded for his merits.

Ajax appears to be associated with: not being duly rewarded for significant effort, struggle, or the display of great courage; experiencing ingratitude for one's own sacrifice, while understanding the reasons somewhere deep within; setbacks; something one desires deeply but falls just short; misfortune just before the end; overcoming obstacles just before the conclusion of a process or project, or enduring disappointment to complete it nonetheless; unexpected last-minute adjustments. Ajax seems to need to learn to do something without expectation, purely for the sake of doing it well, driven by love. It needs to let go of the inclination to do things for the sake of honor, status, or reward and learn to disregard this tendency like a samurai. Within this intricate Trojan energy, a profound opportunity for authentic soul aristocracy unfolds. This is magnificently and miraculously symbolized by the conjunction of the discovery Sun with Sophrosyne in Leo – radiating through selfless actions performed without expecting anything in return from others.

The orbital period is 12 years and 80 days.

10247 AMPHIARAOS

Overcoming a schizoid spiritual attitude by discovering the personal god; spiritually pragmatic opportunism; navigating through the wrong environment and leaving it behind

L4 Trojan discovered on September 24, 1960, by Cornelis Johannes van Houten, Ingrid van Houten-Groeneveld, and Tom Gehrels. The diameter ranges between 15 and 38 km. The name Amphiaraos comes from the Greek ἀμφί (amphi), which has multiple meanings: on both sides, in all directions, surrounding, about, nearly. Where 'amphi' is connected to ἀράομαι (araomai), meaning worship, which is related to ἀρά (ara), prayer. However, this word was frequently used in a malevolent context, invoking a curse or prayer for destructive purposes, and then the word is related to αρη (are), ruin, destruction. Also, see the name Ares, the Greek god of war. Amphiaraos is translated either as doubly cursed (by Ares) or twice as Ares. The interpretation of Amphiaraos seems to involve the blending of spirituality with opportunistic pragmatism and the transition from prayer to magic.

There is a dark, dangerous, and destructive element in Amphiaraos due to its discovery position in the 29th degree of Pisces in very close conjunction with the disaster star Scheat, opposite Taurinensis/Circe/M87; square 1999 RA215. Descriptions: by hook or by crook; tenacity that causes the loss of the starting point; getting involved with the wrong environment or the wrong atmosphere; stepping out at the last moment from a wrong environment that would otherwise have led to downfall, through a constructive, renewed insight, or rather an inspiration that seems to come from the guardian angel; exchanging angels for daemones when the result is lacking; black magic, destructive magic (bane magic), or working with earth spirits; exposure to dangers related to alcohol, water, or drugs.

The key with Amphiaraos is that the deformation of yang energy lies in reacting too much instead of creating and in waiting instead of acting, based on what every great master in the magical realm calls the contact with the personal god. The author of the *Book of Abramelin* calls this the contact with the personal guardian angel, which is essentially the higher self mixed with the true nature of the current incarnation. Everyone has a personal god, which is only found when one looks beyond religious, fear-inducing, dualism-promoting clichés and sees their own tree in the forest. See also Franz Bardon on this. Without contact with one's personal god, one never enters their unique flow, from which all decisions are correct, and choosing between prayers to angels or chthonic beings becomes utterly obsolete.

The orbital period is 11 years and 340 days.

5652 AMPHIMACHUS

Merging strategy with diplomacy; the cost of a battle so high that the struggle only results in loss and ruin; dissonance between fighting on two fronts

Amphimachus was discovered by Eugene and Carolyn Shoemaker on April 24, 1992. The essence of Amphimachus is that a battle, even one compelled, fought for a noble cause or for justice, or truth-seeking, can cause someone to fuse so deeply with the theonic aspect of Mars energy that the human scope can no longer handle this energy. The forces in the human psyche and theonic and archetypal forces, especially concerning Mars-like energies, are a life-threatening match.

Even when well-positioned Amphimachus easily transcends the human limit, ending in pure destruction; Damocles is conjunct Bateman in the discovery chart. A Mars afflicted by Asbolus is in a trine with Pluto/Varda. Eris *(fighting to the extreme)* is conjunct Sethos *(curse)*; sextile Typhon *(infighting)*; opposite Thereus *(wild, untamed, brute force)*. Even a battle that begins for self-defense, justice, or resisting repression can easily derail into a nightmare. Amphimachus is only meaningful as a detector and should only be expressed through diplomatic or non-direct confrontational means.

Characteristics: merging strategy with diplomacy; a point that, when activated, gives two different types of resentment or conflict that dissonantly relate to each other; the cost of a battle so high that the struggle only results in loss and ruin; starting a war on two fronts or ending up in between and becoming a victim of it; succumbing to the battle.

The name Amphimachus means battle on two fronts, on all fronts, or surrounded by battle. The Greek μαχη (mache) means battle. This is the most destructive and dangerous force in a horoscope. An aspect with Amphimachus toxifies the object (planet or asteroid) it contacts in a hazardous manner. The Trojan is most tricky in Cancer and Scorpio due to the emotionality of these signs.

The orbital period is 11 years and 325 days.

4946 ASKALAPHUS
Integrity dissonance; being penalized for rightfully addressing something

L4 Trojan, discovered by Carolyn Shoemaker on January 21, 1981, with a diameter of 57 km, named after the mythical Askalaphos. There exists an Askalaphos who, as the son of Ares and Astyoche, participates in the Trojan War until he is killed by Deiphobos. However, the interpretation of the asteroid Askalaphus in the natal chart seems to align with the other Askalaphos; an underworld god with the specific task of protecting Hades' orchard. One day, he saw Persephone eating a pomegranate, which he reported to the other gods. Persephone had violated a prohibition and, as a result, had to spend 4 (later 6) months in the underworld each year. Her mother Demeter was so enraged that she buried Askalaphos under a heavy rock. Eventually, he was freed by Heracles, but Demeter transformed Askalaphos into an owl, a bird considered an omen of misfortune.

In the natal chart, Askalaphus symbolizes the combination of addressing something and being penalized for it, leading to (social) isolation, while many appreciate that what needed to be addressed was brought to light—a situation most whistleblowers go through. Julian Assange has Askalaphus in the 26th degree of Pisces, including a trine to Mercury/Logos in Cancer; a trine to Jupiter/Sparks/Susansmith/1999 TD10; a square to Venus/Hylonome; and an opposition to Pluto/Pelion. Askalaphus's dilemma seems to revolve around a dissonance between a sense of duty to the law and the 'all too human' aspect. The

FRANC·PARM·INV·
AEN·VIC·PARM·F
M·D·XLVIII·CON
PRIVILEG·VEN

Trojan can create highly complex situations in which one must choose between the damage and risks that demanding integrity from law enforcement and the government brings and the practical consequences for private life and loved ones in the face of the naturally and spontaneously felt ethical duty to address wrongdoing. Similar to Laocoön, Askalaphus raises the question of whether there are not some significant flaws in Creation from a humane standpoint.

The orbital period is 12 years and 90 days.

1871 ASTYANAX

Inner doubt or uncertainty regarding one's identity, displayed very radically to the outside world; becoming the scapegoat, being sacrificed, eliminated, or dismissed because one is perceived as a threat

L5 Trojan, discovered on March 24, 1971, by Cornelis Johannes van Houten, Ingrid van Houten-Groeneveld, and Tom Gehrels. Astyanax comes from a combination of the Greek words ἄστυ (astu) or (asty) city and αναξ (anax) master, lord, chief, thus meaning something like Lord of the City. Astyanax was the son of Hector and Andromache, thrown from the city wall at the behest of Odysseus because he thought Astyanax might display the same formidable combativeness as his already murdered father Hector.

Unlike most Jupiter Trojans, Astyanax's issues are not so much intrinsic but are mainly the result of challenging aspects. Astyanax per se indicates a pleasant, predominantly happy nature, with a good business sense and care for the family. Other qualities are Venus-Libra-Neptune-like; diplomatic, strong in interpersonal relationships, enjoying the more refined aspects of life, artistic or musically talented. The Trojan is also favorable for popularity. However, poor aspecting can manifest behaviors resembling a Taurus who has lost all certainty, with an explosion of destructive yang-energy. This is very exceptional, though. Usually, the Astyanax drama manifests as inner doubt or uncertainty about one's identity, displayed very radically to the outside world, making it difficult for others to react or place it. This can also involve sexual aspects, as Astyanax in a male horoscope can either stimulate homosexuality or a need for anal sex in moments of mental exhaustion (discovery Sun trine Neptune and trine Chrisodom, exactly at their midpoint, in Aries).

Additional associations with this Trojan include becoming the scapegoat, being sacrificed, eliminated, or dismissed because one is perceived as a threat or projecting issues onto someone with a dominant Astyanax that do not align; skin or liver problems; mayoralty.

The orbital period is 12 years and 63 days.

14791 ATREUS
Twelve accidents, thirteen dramas on the relational level, and having to learn a lot here; the feeling of carrying an ancestral curse; sublime insight into good and evil

This L4 Trojan, discovered on September 19, 1973, by Cornelis Johannes van Houten, Ingrid van Houten-Groeneveld, and Tom Gehrels. Atreus is usually viewed in a negative light and initially has something of a raw, malevolent Centaur, whose impulses always turn against themselves in hindsight. Named after the mythical Mycenaean king Atreus, Atreus seems to cast a curse and accentuate all the negative traits of the planet it aspects.

Atreus stimulates the unethical, cruel, rebellious against the law. It also gives the feeling of carrying an ancestral curse or the need to atone for major sins from a previous incarnation through ethical behavior or numerous harsh life lessons. In a positive sense, Atreus provides sublime insight into good and evil and the human role in it. The majority of the misery, problems, and positive development associated with Atreus unquestionably involve the relational and social aspects.

At the time of discovery, Atreus was in the 4th degree of Aries conjunct Heracles and still within the influence of the star Deneb Kaitos *(limitations, misfortune, self-inflicted harm through brute force)*; opposition to Pluto in Libra; square Saturn in Cancer. Venus is so heavily aspected that the refined, gentle qualities are completely overridden by pure lustful satisfaction. A strong Atreus will, therefore, lead to 12 accidents, 13 dramas on the relational level, and require much learning. There is a significant risk with Atreus of facing relational problems related to the repayment or location of the residence. Capricorn qualities play a significant role in this Trojan, forcing the elimination of negative traits of this sign, such as conservatism, taking oneself too seriously, emotional coldness, and status sensitivity. Clear thinking and action emerge when fearlessness is embraced.

The orbital period is 11 years and 242 days.

13184 AUGEIAS

Mental clutter that becomes a burden; the 'clutter' that accumulates, literally or figuratively; that which is only baggage but you keep holding on to; the big cleanup; letting energy flow again by cleaning up

L4 Trojan, discovered on October 4, 1996, by Eric Walter Elst. The location and aspecting of Augeias indicate where and in what situation one tends to let oneself be overrun, where things accumulate, where clutter forms, where or how one can create mess, ultimately losing control, making one's own behavior or sloppiness invade one's life, making everyday life heavier than necessary because unnecessary clutter (material, mental, or emotional) remains, takes up space, suffocates, and blocks the flow of energy. In Gemini, for example, one might lose control due to paper clutter, intellectual projects, excessive communication (including addiction to social media), overdue administration, etc. In Libra, it could be too many relationships, contacts, and in Aries, an excess of activities.

The Augeias conflict resolves by clarifying what one truly wants, adopting a realistic first-things-first policy, identifying real needs, and keeping redundant information and side issues separate from what is immediately necessary. Augeias in Pisces, when afflicted, must question whether so many shoes are really necessary for vacation. Interestingly, the mythic Augeias is inseparably linked to his stables filled to the brim with cow dung, which Hercules cleansed by letting a river flow through them.

This Trojan, according to the discovery chart, has a connection to scatting and related disgusts via Cacus *(dung)* conjunct Messalina *(sexually insatiable)/* Chrisodom *(anal sex)*, and the provocative Centaur 1999 XX143. Moreover, the underlying drive in Augeias, with both lunar nodes in Libra, leans toward creating harmony.

Forensically, Augeias refers to everything where clutter, waste, or filth accumulates, or where a buildup of residue occurs, for example, in sinks or drainage pipes. Augeias can also symbolize people carrying unnecessary emotional or mental baggage or the clutter on a computer hard drive that is not needed but only takes up space.

The orbital period is 11 years and 242 days.

7641 CTEATUS

Enforcement either physically or mentally, verbally or otherwise communicative into something; burglary; breaking something open by brute force; assault, rape; making a political or strategic bypass behind the screens; hard power struggles

Cteatus, with the provisional designation 1986 TT6, stands as a substantial L4 Jupiter Trojan situated in the Greek camp, boasting a diameter of approximately 70 kilometers. This D-type asteroid, discovered by Slovak astronomer Milan Antal on October 5, 1986, at the Toruń Centre for Astronomy in Piwnice, Poland, is characterized by its dark surface and notably inclined orbit, along with an extended rotation period of 27.8 hours, surpassing the average. As one of the 50 largest Jupiter Trojans, it finds its namesake in Greek mythology, honoring Cteatus, the conjoined twin and father of Amphimachus.

When this asteroid holds prominence in an astrological chart, particularly in precise conjunction with celestial bodies such as the Sun, Mars, Moon, ascendant, DC, Uranus, Pluto, or Eris, it may exert a potentially perilous influence.

The discovery chart indicates tendencies toward boundary-crossing behavior with a strong inclination toward violence or, conversely, becoming a victim of such behavior. With the discovery-Sun on Algol conjunct Phaeton *(going off course)*, Mars conjunct 1999 RA215 *(attacks)*, and Eris *(never give in or up)* square Amycus *(power abuse)*, this already constitutes intense energy. However, the crux lies in the Mercury aspect. Mercury *(thought, mentality)* is conjunct 2002 KX14 *(unstable; wanting to eliminate something or someone; arbitrary)*. Positioned in the third degree of Scorpio, Mercury forms an exact sextile with Makemake *(peak performances)/* Nessus *(assault, intrusion)/* Thereus *(employing gross violence or brute force)* in Virgo and 2001 SQ73 *(engage in discussion, fluctuating or pulsating bulging energy)* in Capricorn. Mercury thus illuminates the midpoint of the objects with which it forms a sextile. Furthermore, Mercury is in an exact trine with Neptune, which can either save the situation *(inclination towards directing, photographing, or writing about violent crimes)* or exacerbate it when drugs or alcohol fill the Neptune sphere. Forensically, Cteatus may also indicate violence, tension, quarrels, or sudden blackouts of the electricity network.

The orbital period is 11 years and 332 days.

1867 DEIPHOBUS

Facilitator of one's individuation process; learning to shield and thus allow the flourishing of one's uniqueness, authenticity, and individuality

Large D-type L5 Trojan, discovered on March 3, 1971, by Carlos Ulrrico Cesco and Arturo G. Samuel, with a diameter of almost 122.7 km. The interpretation primarily points to learning to shield and thus allowing the flourishing of one's uniqueness, authenticity, individuality, integrity, with the main challenge lying in resisting invasion by non-nourishing information, people, or influences, including obsessors. In summary, Deiphobus serves as a facilitator of one's individuation process (discovery position in the 2nd degree of Virgo, conjunct uncorrected Black Moon).

The story of Roald Dahl about a man living just outside a village applies to Deiphobus. He would bring home any sick, malnourished, or injured animal he encountered. One day, the villagers, having heard nothing from him for a long time, went to check on him at his cottage, only to discover that the animals had consumed him.

The orbital period is 11 years and 233 days.

18493 DEMOLEON

Transforming aggression into positive assertiveness through aligning ideals with feasibility; occult interests; promiscuity in love life; talent for networking and group cohesion; stab wound to the face; chest injuries

L5 Trojan, discovered on April 17, 1996, by Eric Walter Elst. Demoleon combines high sensitivity, a talent for networking and group cohesion with an excessively heightened combativeness, often resulting in a farce or deformed output in the mentioned areas. Particularly challenging is the impact on the love life, where the tendency toward promiscuity is so high that individuals with a strong Demoleon should question the practicality of a stable relationship. Yet, Demoleon is also divided in this aspect, given the trine to Juno in the discovery chart. There is only one type of partner suitable for a dominant Demoleon, and that is the Pisces type with an interest in the mystical, occult, or astrology.

Somehow, Demoleon must find a way to synergize conflicting forces and talents. In the context of deranged Mars/Aries energy, this always boils down to transforming aggression into positive assertiveness. Particularly here, this process is facilitated by a reality check, evaluating all ideals, desires, and concepts against their feasibility or the possibility of realizing them within a given timeframe and with available resources.

Demoleon was positioned in the 12th degree of Scorpio during its discovery and is strongly influenced by the star Acrux *(magic, ceremonies, mysteries, astrology)*. Demoleon means Lion of the People, a combination of the Greek words δημος (demos) the people, the populace, and λεων (leon) lion. In contrast to Demophon, Demoleon is a poor populist, and the voice of the people only expresses indignation aloud, which others only dare to think secretly. Forensically, especially in Fire signs or martial asteroids, Demoleon has a connection with facial injuries caused by a sharp metal object or a knife, and there is also a link between chest injuries related to wrongly directed brute force. Mythically, there is a battle in the Trojan War, but also a centaur Demoleon in the conflict between centaurs and Lapiths. He kills Crantor by shattering his chest armor with a thrown log. However, the wounded chest appears to have a rebound effect on the Jupiter-Trojan Demoleon. In women's charts, Demoleon makes them verbally resilient to aggressive, often too harsh towards children.

The orbital period is 12 years and 73 days.

4057 DEMOPHON

That which aligns your vision or specialty with knowledge or idealism, to connect with a group of people and thus appears to represent them; populism

L4 Trojan, discovered on October 15, 1984, by Edward Bowell with a diameter of 71 km. Demophon means the voice of the people. The discovery Sun of Demophon is in the 23rd degree of Libra, forming a trine with Varuna in Gemini *(significant communicative and connecting impact)*; trine with (2007 OR10) Snow White in Aquarius *(group feeling and group idealism)*; sextile with Hylonome *(great popularity)*. Demophon itself was positioned in the 21st degree of Aries at the time of discovery, conjunct Cruithne. Characteristics: that which aligns your vision or specialty with knowledge or idealism to connect with a group of people and thus appears to represent them; populism. Forensically: demagogues, populists; idealistic leaders or spokespersons for groups.

The orbital period is 12 years and 41 days.

1437 DIOMEDES

Being able to plan and organize contextually, establishing an organization; success comes after calibrating goals according to inner growth needs; startups

L4 Trojan of 284 × 126 × 65 km, discovered on August 3, 1937, by Karl Wilhelm Reinmuth. Diomedes is a combination of Διος (Dios) god, here Zeus, and μηδομαι (medomai), which refers to thinking in the form of planning. There is a Greek warrior Diomedes in the Trojan War and a mythical Diomedes who threw people to flesh-eating horses. Diomedes, as an exception to most Trojans, has a discovery chart where feminine energy plays a greater role. The discovery Sun is in the 11th degree of Leo, but, among others, conjunct Haumea and Elst-Pizarro; square Sila-Nunam and trine Salacia; opposition 1995 SM55. Epona *(horses)* is conjunct Tisiphone *(retribution)*. Diomedes itself was positioned in the 4th degree of Pisces at the time of discovery.

Diomedes is associated with planning, organizing, establishing an expanding organization that can achieve significant proportions. The yang deformation here involves setting clear objectives. Initially, someone with a dominant Diomedes may lack this, until, through trial and error, it becomes clear that Diomedes' full power comes to fruition when the projected idea, which is the blueprint for a growth organization, is in synergy and alignment with what one seeks for inner satisfaction. Diomedes is exceptionally context-sensitive, acting as a catalyst in the maturation of Diomedes' potential. Forensically: startups; emerging companies still in the fresh creative stage; consultants assisting entrepreneurs with the start; demiurgic processes and demiurgic stages of processes (in magical or theurgical contexts).

The orbital period is 11 years and 266 days.

2148 EPEIOS

Scorpionic nature; very calculating with a tendency toward evil; military engineering; in-fighting, breaking in, conquering terrain; bonding anxiety in which the lack of love and intimacy prompts a person to engage in activities within an evil construct; irrationally critical of paranormal or spiritual conceptions and appearances; great diplomatic or manipulative skills

Epeios, a mid-sized L4 Jupiter Trojan hailing from the Greek camp, boasts an estimated diameter of approximately 38 kilometers. The Danish astronomer Richard Martin West first spotted this dark Jovian asteroid on October 24, 1976, at ESO's La Silla Observatory in northern Chile. Designated as the central celestial body within the proposed Epeios family, this asteroid derives its name from the mythological figure Epeius.

In the realm of Greek mythology, Epeios, the son of Panopeus, emerged as a craftsman and soldier who fought alongside the Greeks during the Trojan War. His notable victories include a boxing match against Euryalo during the Patroclus Memorial Games, where he emerged triumphant. Later, in the Achilles Memorial Games, he faced off against Akamas, the son of Theseus. Epeios's enduring claim to fame, however, lies in his role as the mastermind behind the construction of the iconic wooden Trojan horse. Collaborating with Odysseus, who had received divine guidance from Pallas Athene in a dream, Epeios crafted the horse, its secret hatch known only to him. Legend has it that Epeios even concealed himself within the Trojan horse during its fateful journey to Troy. Upon returning from the war, Epeios, in various accounts, either founded the city of Metapontion or Pisa upon landing in Italy. Notably, within the temple of Argos, two ancient wooden sculptures, believed to be Epeios's handiwork, depicted the divine figures Aphrodite and Hermes.

Someone with a dominant Epeios has a cunning, strategic, and diplomatic Scorpio-like nature with a Saturnine influence (discovery-Sun conjunct Arawn (sober Saturn-like Plutino) / Tezcatlipoca *(dark magic)* / Nyx *(nocturnal, the intrinsically unfinished process)*. Such a person is very calculating and will rarely lose patience, giving in to aggressive emotional outbursts. (Eris conjunct Okyrhoe). The Sun also forms an exact trine with 2001 QG298 *(extreme power desire; behind-the-scenes networks)* and squares 2002 TX300 *(bully, criminal)* in Aquarius and squares Neoptolemus *(start conflict or war)* in 2 degrees Leo. During discovery, Epeios was in the 9th degree Leo conjunct Amphimachus *(merging diplomacy with strategy)*, trine Plutino 1998 VG44 *(official state lies consolidation)*, opposition Hilda *(energy draining)* / Lempo *(metaphysics)* / sextile Varuna *(big media event, big recorded event)*. Mars is conjunct Ixion *(Frankenstein technology)* / Toro *(brute force flying off course)*, opposition Typhon *(fighting, persisting until you're in)*. Mercury is conjunct Pelion *(will-recreation)*; sextile Makemake/Zhulong *(diplomatic top-skills)*.

There is a strong temptation for this Trojan to turn to evil. In a positive astrological environment, the opposite can also occur, and Epeion can become a masterful evil fighter. However, the primary tendency of this asteroid is towards the dark side. Attachment issues can play a significant role, often decisive in leading someone to the wrong side of the line (Venus in Sagittarius in an exact square with Athropos/Psyche, opposition Ceto). Uranus is conjunct Varda *(deal a blow, make a point)* / 2001 SQ73 *(pulsating inflated energy, tendency for debate)* and trine Nessus *(intrusion, assault)*.

Forensically, Epeios lives up to his mythical name (builder of the Trojan horse) as the military engineer or manipulator as a profession resonates most with the essence of this Trojan. Epeios can also indicate inventions that are purposeful but lack lateral context intelligence, ultimately causing more harm and suffering than they have been beneficial.

The orbital period is 11 years and 332 days.

23382 EPISTROPHOS
Retreating movements, withdrawal; reality checks

L4 Trojan, discovered on September 30, 1973, by Cornelis Johannes van Houten, Ingrid van Houten-Groeneveld, and Tom Gehrels, named after Epistrophos of Phocis.

The interpretation of Epistrophos is not simply about returning or making a U-turn. The Trojan gives the impulse to withdraw from the elements with which Epistrophos interacts (degree, sign, house, aspects). However, this withdrawal is not an evasion but part of a sublimation process, where progress (proodos) undergoes a reality check concerning both the self-integrity and authenticity of the person in question and the current reality.

Ultimately, this crystallization process unfolds, leading to the right actions and achievements. The maturity of Epistrophos is achieved when the right balance is found between what the Sufis call Kadar (small will) and Kaza (Great Will), creating one's unique flow with unique talents. There is a significant Aries/Pisces dichotomy in this Trojan that needs to be transformed into Aries/Pisces synergy, as well as a keen instinct for striking while the iron is hot.

The orbital period is 11 years and 322 days.

624 HECTOR

Pride or authority challenged by a talented and relentless adversary; clinging to an absolutism that overrides human reasoning; the necessity of perspective; tenacity; ambition and drive; mundanely significant invasions

L4 Trojan discovered on February 10, 1907, by August Kopff, with dimensions of 363 by 207 km. Hector is the largest of all discovered Jupiter Trojans. Initially, Hector signifies a persistence to the point of holding on, often against better judgment or the laws of reality. The Trojan also instills high ambition and drive. Personal pride or authority is challenged by a talented and relentless adversary (Discovery-Hector in the 21st degree of Leo opposite Sun/Amycus/Talent). This tenacity is neutral in itself, and whether this trait manifests in favor or against the individual depends on their maturity.

However, Hector carries the danger of stubbornly adhering to an absolutism that overrides human reasoning, leading to unnecessary chaos for oneself and the surroundings (Pluto/Alu opposite AMOS). Additionally, Hector inherently possesses the ability to bind a group to itself (Venus conjunct Snow White) and remains popular with that group. Hector can inspire courage, perseverance, and produce a winner, with the lurking risk that the achieved goal may not be a true victory if the situation emotionally or ethically no longer aligns. In combination with many soft planets or the right harmonious aspects in the horoscope, Hector can be a significant asset.

Jesse Owens had Hector conjunct Varuna *(grow big, super-event)*; sextile Admetos (unyielding in this aspect). In conjunction or hard aspects with malefic planets, this Trojan can become a disaster for oneself and the surroundings when clinging to a creed or absolutism turns into mass psychosis. Hector must cultivate positive Leo forces *(warmth, creativity, earned authority, constructive and nurturing leadership)* and reject negative Gemini traits *(manipulative communication, short-sighted arguments, lack of backbone)* to remain positive.

Forensic significance: politicians rallying a group to execute destructive or warlike policies; humiliation after death; very significant invasions with lasting media impact. On the day Hitler began his invasion of Poland (September 1, 1939), Hector was decile Polonia (decile = a preference for something – here invading Poland – directly linked to a tangible event).

The orbital period is 11 years and 350 days.

1872 HELENOS

Clairvoyance, visionary abilities, foresight, experiencing problems due to or suffering from these abilities

L5 Trojan, discovered on March 24, 1971, by Cornelis Johannes van Houten, Ingrid van Houten-Groeneveld, and Tom Gehrels. The interpretation points to clairvoyance, visionary abilities, foresight, and experiencing problems due to these abilities.

My son has Helenos conjunct Micromegas in 16 Aquarius; a trine to Black Moon in Libra; sextile a conjunction of the asteroid Lilith with Hidalgo in Sagittarius, and opposition to 1997CR29 *(vision, crystallization, inner knowing)* – against a backdrop of Moon square Neptune and strongly aspected Flammario, Illapa, and 2001UR163. As a child, he was so strongly clairvoyant that he suffered greatly. He saw the spirits of the dead, often those of a deceased girl who troubled him, as well as Elementals and auras. However, it has made his mind much richer and stronger because he knows that reality is much larger than officially recognized. When he was about 3 years old, he saw a small creature that was busy all the time at his window (Micromegas = little people). Most likely, Helenos indicates an ongoing love-hate relationship with the astral world, keeping communication with it always in the background and peaking from time to time in extraordinary experiences.

The orbital period is 12 years and 67 days.

30698 HIPPOKOON

Knowledge of horses, situations involving horses; strong desire for personal development or physical improvement; fear or concern about the future; dichotomy between preserving one's individuality and entering into relationships or partnerships; singles

L5 Trojan, discovered on October 16, 1977, by Cornelis Johannes van Houten, Ingrid van Houten-Groeneveld, and Tom Gehrels. Hippokoon means horse-knower. During the discovery, Hippokoon was in the 20th degree of Aries septile *(fascination aspect)* Epona *(horses)*. The interpretation indeed points to horses, knowledge of horses, situations involving horses, but also a strong desire for personal development or physical improvement, especially during transits related to these themes. Hippokoon also makes individuals ambitious and imparts a pronounced aversion to socializing or entering into partnerships if the conditions require too much adjustment, demand concessions that one does not support, or if one has to sacrifice too much of one's own life.

There is often a chronic underlying fear or concern about the future, and individuals with Hippokoon may sense certain future events or developments in advance. Lastly, Hippokoon harbors an intense inner conflict that becomes more pronounced over the years. This conflict explicitly revolves around a dichotomy between a strong desire to maintain individual freedom and the social compromises that entering a relationship, partnership, or collaboration inevitably entails. Either one manages to establish a satisfying synergy, or one chooses the existence of eternal singledom, with or without resentment towards the opposite gender. Forensically, it is associated with the world of horse enthusiasts and experts; singles; people who align with apocalyptic visions of the future and futurology.

The orbital period is 11 years and 327 days.

13387 IRUS

Expressing strong opinions based on incorrect premises, or puncturing through the certainty of others; accumulating bad karma by saying or writing wrong things; rejection-acceptance issues

Irus is an L4 Trojan, discovered on December 22, 1998, by the Osservatorio Astronomico di Farra d'Isonzo. Irus was named after Iros, a beggar/messenger in Homer's Odyssey, who was later killed by Odysseus.

The characteristics of Irus include: asserting something with great certainty; being firm on an incorrect basis – being ill-prepared and relying on an idea that is incorrect, or knowing it's incorrect but going along with the consensus opinion or assuming that people won't bother to fact-check; facing problems due to one's own certainty or emphasis; misplaced or misjudged assertiveness.

Forensically, it can also refer to a beggar, messenger, or assertive individual. Bill Clinton, who vehemently claimed during the Lewinsky affair, "I did NOT have sex with that woman!" has Irus in the 21st degree of Sagittarius in the 3rd house, conjunct Elatus/Sophrosyne *(smooth-talking the situation because he thought he should)* opposing Uranus/Orcus/Logos in Sagittarius in the 9th house *(an equally bizarre and lethal expression of hypocrisy with no hint of credibility)*.

The orbital period is 11 years and 348 days.

4707 KHRYSES, CHRYSES

Sublimation, highest quality standards; aiming for perfection; giving everything for a cause; power and wealth; love spoiled by money or a marriage of convenience; subtle toxicity; space weather

Khryses, also known as Chryses, is an L5 Trojan discovered on August 13, 1988, by Carolyn Shoemaker. The name is derived from the Greek χρυσεος (chryseos), meaning golden or made of gold. In Greek mythology, Khryses was the father of Chryseis, who was abducted by Agamemnon during the Trojan War.

Characteristics: Khryses embodies the essence of sublimation and the pursuit of the highest quality. It reflects the desire to complete or leave something perfect, giving one's all for a superior result, striving for perfection, providing something of superior authority or quality. It is associated with power and wealth. However, it also symbolizes the potential for love to be tainted by money or financial marriages, carrying an undercurrent of toxicity.

At the time of discovery, Khryses was found conjunct the highly favorable star Achernar. The distortion of yang-energy in Khryses may manifest through the blinding effects of perfectionism, stringent quality standards, and the impact of wealth on social and love life. Obtaining wealth through questionable means or export trade is another facet to consider. Perfect things can act as black holes on the soul.

Forensically, Khryses is linked to the parents of abducted children or things made of gold and space weather, encompassing phenomena such as solar flares, solar winds, electromagnetic storms, and the auroras (borealis and australis).

The orbital period is 11 years and 288 days.

3240 LAOCOÖN

Perceiving what no one sees and no one wants to see, addressing it with good intentions and concern, only to be punished for it; hyperawareness; the betrayal of the gods versus the birth of Heka; a Promethean spirit; Promethean drama and injustice

Laocoön, is a L5-Trojan, discovered on November 7, 1978, by Eleanor Helen and Schelte Bus, emerges as a celestial enigma. Named after the Trojan Apollo priest Laocoön, this heavenly body parallels the biblical figure of Job, evoking contemplation from psychologists, theologians, and philosophers alike.

L.J.S.

In the Homeric epics, Laocoön's absence is noted, but Virgil's Aeneid captures his immortal words of warning: "Equo ne credite, Teucri. Quidquid id est, timeo Danaos et dona ferentes". ("Do not trust the horse, Trojans. Whatever it is, I fear the Greeks, even when they bring gifts".) Laocoön's myth unfolds as he discerns Odysseus' cunning ploy. Despite convincing most of his fellow citizens, his fate takes a dark turn as the Greek Sinon introduces doubt. A gruesome omen, two serpents emerge from the sea to consume Laocoön and his sons.

Laocoön, embodying Jupiter-Trojan, encapsulates the most complex Trojan and a profound human dilemma. Philosophers, from Nietzsche to existentialists, grapple with the complexities mirrored in Laocoön's narrative. Only the ancient Egyptians offer an answer: Heka. His sharp intellect and human concern are rewarded with treacherous betrayal by the gods, notably Athena, the goddess of wisdom.

Laocoön unveils the inherent flaws in creation, showcasing the human suffering devoid of rationality, stemming from collective madness, jealousy, scapegoating, hatred, and media manipulation. As depicted in the documentary HOME, the planet faces destruction by corporations and political powers, while war's irrationality persists. The Egyptians viewed gods as natural forces, permitting priests to counter their influence through rituals and magic.

Laocoön's journey prompts an offensive for human autonomy against obsessions and obsessors. With the discovery Sun opposing Sedna, he sees through the modified reality, opposing challenges to his core. Laocoön was positioned at the 11th degree of Capricorn during discovery, sextile Asbolus, the seer of the gruesome.

The orbital period is 12 years and 19 days.

4792 LYKAON

The lonely wolf mentality, goal-oriented endurance, persisting in pursuing a course despite resistance, setbacks, bad news, or obstacles; a tough undercurrent of optimism and goal-directed self-confidence; poor preparation as the Achilles' heel

L5-Trojan, discovered by Carolyn Shoemaker on September 10, 1988, and named after the Trojan son of King Priam and Laothoe, who was sold as a slave by Achilles but later returned to Troy, only to be killed by Achilles. Characteristics: The lonely wolf mentality, goal-oriented endurance, persisting in pursuing a course despite resistance, setbacks, bad news, or obstacles; a tough undercurrent of optimism and goal-directed self-confidence.

Lykaon has a Ram-like and Mars-Jupiter-like nature. Lykaon's vulnerable point is poor preparation (or collaboration), leading to just missing the goal. There is no lack of energy, purpose, and stamina; however, someone with a dominant Lykaon must learn to dot all the 'i's' to convert their energy into successful endeavors and actions. The development of lateral strategic, planning, and logistical insight is crucial. Forensic implications include people caring for wolves, werewolf themes, and those embodying the lonely wolf archetype.

The orbital period is 12 years and 26 days.

3063 MAKHAON

A complex schizoid nature that must overcome infertile mindsets, persons or other forms of pressure that are hindering personal passion and expression. The solidification of personal power and potential fame is best achieved through artistic endeavors. Forensically: healers, medics

Makhaon is a substantial L4 Jupiter Trojan connected to the Greek camp, boasting a diameter of approximately 114 kilometers. Discovered on August 4, 1983, by Soviet astronomer Lyudmila Karachkina at the Crimean Astrophysical Observatory in Nauchnij on the Crimean peninsula, this dark D-type asteroid serves as the central figure in the proposed Makhaon family. It is among the 20 largest Jupiter Trojans, featuring a rotation period of 8.6 hours. The asteroid's name is inspired by the renowned healer Machaon in Greek mythology.

In Greek mythology, Machaon (Ancient Greek: Μαχάων, romanized: Macháōn), the son of Asclepius and the elder brother of Podalirius, led an army from Tricca in the Trojan War on the side of the Greeks. Described as "... brave, dependable, prudent, patient, and merciful" by Dares the Phrygian, Machaon is also placed as the son of Asclepius, father of Nicomachus, and ancestor of Aristotle, according to Hermippus in *Diogenes Laertius's Lives and Opinions of Eminent Philosophers*. Machaon and Podalirius were esteemed surgeons and medics. In the *Iliad*, Machaon was wounded and incapacitated by Paris, yet he (or his brother) went on to heal Philoctetes, Telephus, and Menelaus after sustaining an arrow at the hand of Pandarus during the war. Additionally, Machaon was believed to possess herbs given to his father Asclepius by Chiron, the centaur. His demise came at the hands of Eurypylus in the tenth year of the war, and he was laid to rest in Gerenia in Messenia, where he became a revered figure among the people.

Despite the mythical association with a healer, when Makhaon is prominent in a personal chart and the overall horoscope or genes indicate artistic talent, such an individual would benefit the most from this Trojan by pursuing a career as an artist or musician. Makhaon possesses a complex schizoid nature, where the inclination towards conservatism is as potent as the need to think and express ideas independently. Subcutaneously, there is a conflict between passion and demands imposed by parents, family, or tradition. Moreover, the nature of Makhaon strongly stimulates a calibration process aimed at solidifying personal power. Neptune in Sagittarius, the planet governing drugs, video, photography, painting, filmmaking, and music, is conjunct Bienor *(fame through personal effort)*, sextile Pluto in Libra, and trines Makemake *(peak performance)* in Leo. Jupiter is trine 200 VE95 *(great artistic talent, drugs; see Herman Brood and Jean-Michel Basquiat)*. The discovery Sun is in Leo, square Varda *(making a point or a hit)* / Arawn (Saturn-like Plutino). In contrast to Arawn, Mercury is square Uranus *(independent, original mentality; rebellious when frustrated)*. This creates an ideal combination for expressionist art once the conflicting energies are brought into synergy. Especially smearing thick layers of paint, epoxy, or other thick substances on canvas (COBRA-style) is favored by this Trojan, thanks to the opposition Augeias-Sun. Makhaon was at its discovery in 22 Aquarius conjunct Menelaus.

Forensically, Makhaon continues to symbolize a healer, medical specialist, or medic within a military occupation. Initially, there might seem to be no apparent link between the artist and the medic. However, healing fundamentally involves freeing flow from blockages. Consequently, the restoration of flow serves as the connection between great art and successful healing.

The orbital period is 11 years and 327 days.

1647 MENELAUS

Extreme sexual activity, interests, curiosities, quests, experiments, challenges, and scope

L4-Trojan discovered on June 23, 1957, by Seth Nicholsen, with a diameter of 42.23 km. The name is derived from the Greek Menelaos, a combination of *meno* (to withstand, resist) and *laos* (the people).

Menelaus is a highly sexual Trojan, positioned at the time of discovery between the stars Kuma (in the mouth of Draco) and Alwaid or Rastaban in the 11th degree of Sagittarius. Traditionally, this zone is considered toxic or poisonous. Menelaus was conjunct Machiavelli *(power)* and opposite Phaeton *(thrown out of orbit due to excessive speed)*.

Characteristics include extreme sexual activity, interests, curiosities, quests, experiments, challenges, and scope, etc. The underlying drive is toward intensity, primarily sought in the sexual realm. Sexual asteroids are often also highly artistic because libido energy underlies both sex and art. There is a tendency in Menelaus to want to proclaim or emancipate something from the sexual (or artistic) realm when it comes to taboos. In a negative setting, Menelaus's sexuality can be poisonous, energy-draining, and destructive.

The orbital period is 11 years and 332 days.

3451 MENTOR

A teacher, an exemplar in intellectual development; an enormous urge to transmit something for a fresh start in a new phase of life

L5-Trojan with a diameter of 90 km, discovered on April 19, 1984, by Antonín Mrkos. Mentor is named after Odysseus's friend, who, during his absence, kept an eye on the suitors around Penelope, supported his son, and was regularly assisted by Pallas Athena with clever insights.

In personal horoscopy, Mentor signifies a mentor, a teacher, an exemplar in intellectual development. This can be a currently active person, a writer who serves as a mentor through their legacy, or a spirit that aids in inspiration. A strongly placed Mentor instills an immense desire to impart something that can lead to a fresh start in a new phase of life or to enter a new, improved phase and broaden horizons. Mentor fosters sensitivity and possesses good qualities for collaboration. However, Mentor's yang deformation relates to improperly dosed attention or a didactically incorrect way of setting an example, which may lead Mentor to exhibit parasitic traits. In this sense, the other or a student may find it challenging to break free from this example. Taoist masters resolve this by providing a pupil with only 10% of their knowledge as a standard and allowing them to figure out the rest themselves.

Forensically: a mentor, teacher; a spouse or life partner who has become or is becoming very wealthy through trade, communication, publishing, or the writing profession.

The orbital period is 11 years and 186 days.

2260 NEOPTOLEMUS
Initiating a battle or war; devising an argument to start a battle or war; false flag strategies

L4-Trojan with a diameter of 71.7 km, discovered on November 26, 1975, by the Purple Mountain Observatory in China. The discovery Sun is in the 4th degree of Sagittarius, conjunct 1999 TD10 *(invasion)*; trine Saturn in Leo; trine corrected Black Moon in Aries; square 1992 QB1 *(thus not building bridges, but actively and purposefully invading)*. Neoptolemus itself was positioned in the 27th degree of Gemini during discovery.

From the Greek Νεοπτολεμος (Neoptolemos), Neoptolemus means new war. The characteristics seem to fully conform to this: initiating a battle or war; seeking conflict; devising an argument to start a battle or war.

Barack Obama – who during his presidency bombed seven countries and daily signed a list from the CIA containing people to be killed by drones for the military-industrial complex and the U.S. economy that largely depends on it – has Neoptolemus *(initiating a battle or war)* nearly exactly conjunct Eris *(struggle to the extreme)* and conjunct Chaos *(Plutonian compulsion causing chaos)*, Hilda *(negativity)*, Utopia *(delusion)*, and Aphrodite *(covering with charm; Nobel Peace Prize)*, opposite TRIUMF *(triumph that is not triumph)*; square Toro *(brutal explosive violence)*. Hillary Clinton, who just before the 2017 elections was pushing for war with Russia and was heavily involved in the mass murders approved by Obama in Libya – and elsewhere – has Neoptolemus conjunct the uncorrected Black Moon in the 20th degree of Capricorn *(deformation)*, opposite Makemake in Cancer *(depopulation)*; trine Echeclus *(the new order)*.

Forensically, Neoptolemus indicates: warmongers; war initiators; politically motivated media nonsense intended to incite support for war; false flag attacks.

The orbital period is 11 years and 303 days.

1143 ODYSSEUS

The development of intense hatred; described as clever, cunning, and resourceful; known for technical expertise and ingenuity, often displaying a knack for ingenious solutions, especially under pressure or in challenging situations; tends to maintain a neutral ethical stance; prone to separation from spouse or partner and child due to anger, conflict, or intense feelings of hatred.

L4-Trojan, discovered on January 28, 1930, by Karl Wilhelm Reinmuth, has a diameter of 126 km. Named after the Greek hero Odysseus, derived from the Greek word meaning 'to hate', this Trojan exhibits a predisposition, particularly when strongly placed, towards developing intense feelings of hatred, sometimes associated with PTSD, as well as demonstrating the legendary resourcefulness of Odysseus. Key attributes include cleverness, cunning, and resourcefulness, often accompanied by technical proficiency. Notably, Odysseus is adept at generating fortunate ideas spontaneously, especially when facing adversity. While typically adopting a morally neutral stance, individuals under the influence of this archetype may experience separation from their spouse or partner and child due to anger, conflict, or intense feelings of hatred.

The manifestation of Odysseus' traits is contingent upon individual attitudes and the overall horoscopic configuration, including progressions and long-term transits. In a positive context, their remarkable resourcefulness shines through, while in a negative environment, feelings of hatred can escalate into destructive obsessions. Addressing the misalignment of yang energy, common among Jupiter Trojans, involves recognizing the potential for constructive as well as destructive outcomes. Overcoming hatred and the impulse to assert dominance over adversaries is crucial for nurturing positive and resourceful behavior. Even amidst feelings of hatred, Odysseus displays remarkable ingenuity in devising retaliatory strategies, prompting reflection on the appropriateness of embracing such inspirations. Forensically, Odysseus symbolism extends to governmental intrusions into privacy through deceitful means, hate-related incidents and crimes, and the experiences of military personnel or individuals separated from their families due to PTSD.

The orbital period is 12 years and 11 days.

2456 PALAMEDES

Popularity, or widespread affection through avenues like photography, videography, painting, writing activities, or publications on blogs or vlogs; individuals who are victims of betrayal or those working in drug enforcement, such as the American DEA, or individuals who may become victims of it. Engaging in the trade of designer drugs; vulnerabilities to sprained ankles and foot-related issues

Palamedes is a substantial L4 Jupiter Trojan, positioned in the Greek camp, with a diameter of around 99.6 kilometers. Discovered on January 30, 1966, by astronomers at the Purple Mountain Observatory in Nanking, China, this C-type asteroid belongs to the 50 largest Jupiter Trojans. It assumes a non-family role within the Jovian background population.

The nomenclature of Palamedes is rooted in Greek mythology, specifically named after the intelligent Greek commander Palamedes of the Trojan War. Palamedes was an Euboean prince and the son of King Nauplius. Renowned for his association with the invention of dice, numbers, and letters, Palamedes's lineage is entwined with various accounts regarding his family. While his mother is identified as either Clymene, Hesione, or Philyra, Palamedes has siblings in Oeax and Nausimedon. Within the drama of the Trojan War, Palamedes emerges as a key figure, yet intriguingly, he finds no mention in Homer's Iliad. Notably, his involvement revolves around retrieving Odysseus from Ithaca after Paris took Helen to Troy. Odysseus, reluctant to uphold his promise, feigned insanity by plowing his fields chaotically with a donkey and an ox. Palamedes, astute to the ruse, strategically placed Odysseus' son, Telemachus, in front of the plow, compelling Odysseus to reveal his sanity. Palamedes' fate varies across ancient sources. According to Hyginus, Odysseus, harboring resentment for Palamedes' interference, orchestrated his demise. Odysseus hid gold in Palamedes' tent and forged a letter from Priam, leading to accusations of treason and Palamedes being stoned to death by the Greeks. Pausanias offers an alternate version where Palamedes met his end during a fishing expedition, drowned by Odysseus and Diomedes. Dictys Cretensis spins yet another tale, recounting how Palamedes, enticed by the promise of treasure, was lured into a well and subsequently crushed by stones. Ironically there were also several astronomical designations that indicated Palamedes before receiving its official name (1966 BA1, 1973 TJ, 1977 AK1 and 1979 EF).

The etymology of the name Palamedes lacks a unanimous interpretation, yet a plausible breakdown reveals that 'pala' signifies spade or shovel, while 'medes' denotes '... son of', suggesting a potential translation as 'Son of the

Spade' or 'Son of the Shovel'. The life of the mythical Palamedes caricatures a benevolently intelligent and advisory individual who, due to seeing through illusions and deceit, faces unfavorable consequences, ultimately paying the price with his life. In a negative light, someone with a prominently placed Palamedes may succumb to betrayal within the realm of trading or producing designer drugs, find themselves unwillingly thrust into the public spotlight due to a scandalous affair, or damage their reputation through reckless, idealistic, and rebellious behavior that certain authorities do not appreciate. Alternatively, frustration-driven attempts to force a more accommodating space may lead to self-inflicted harm. On a positive note, Palamedes can propel someone to fame, popularity, or widespread affection through avenues like photography, videography, painting, writing activities, or publications on blogs or vlogs. This includes erotic photography or art, which need not be overly intricate to generate recognition. A robust but afflicted Palamedes renders one susceptible to injuries and wounds in the ankles, calves, shins, and feet.

Forensically, a robust Palamedes may signify individuals who are victims of betrayal or those working in drug enforcement, such as the American DEA, or individuals who may become victims of it. Engaging in the trade of designer drugs, particularly substances like XTC, is strongly discouraged with an afflicted Palamedes. Physically, there may be vulnerabilities to sprained ankles and foot-related issues.

The orbital period is 11 years and 226 days.

617 PATROCLES-MENOETIUS
Yang energy going off the rails and intensity on the surface; profoundly human inside

Patrocles is a binary L5 Trojan with a diameter of approximately 122 km, discovered on August 17, 1907, by August Kopff. Menoetius, the second body, was discovered on September 22, 2001, measuring 113 km. Both bodies, revolving around each other, together span a space of about 560 km in diameter.

Patrocles comes from the Greek *Patroklos* (Glory of the father). Menoetius or Menoetes means *doomed power* or *pain of power*. Centaurs each create a form of chaos, conflict, wound, or drama, and Jupiter Trojans do the same. However, the drama with Centaurs is based on the out-of-the-box principle. They are outliers, beautifully analogous to their bizarre eccentric elliptical orbits and aphelia-perihelia positions. With Jupiter Trojans, as mentioned earlier, the drama is almost always traceable to unbalanced, and thereby excessive yang energy. The binary Trojan Patrocles pretty much takes the cake in this regard. Jupiter represents the most archetypal yang energy – not Mars, which merely displays the most manifest form. Jupiter Trojans show deformations of yang energy that each Trojan must undergo a unique balancing process.

The interpretation of Patrocles-Menoetius actually points to two outcomes. The most regular one is that of Patrocles-Menoetius as an indicator of a point in the horoscope where yang energy goes off the rails or overwhelms. Due to this high concentration of active and offensive energy, this point in the horoscope becomes a concentric point for forces coming from the aspects that Patrocles-Menoetius makes and the zodiacal position it occupies (including the degree meaning). These forces are as if bundled, strengthened, and 'slinged out', emphasizing it in the overall horoscope. Patrocles-Menoetius thus works like a small vortex. The other outcome is rarer and more dramatic. In this case, Patrocles-Menoetius seems to reflect the myth from the Trojan War, where Patroclus is killed by Hector and Achilles subsequently takes revenge on Hector by killing him and dragging his body around for days behind his horse. The essence of this drama; the death or mistreatment of a person, leading to much new violence, sticks to this Trojan.

The most striking example is given by Mark Andrew Holmes with Rodney King, with Patrocles-Menoetius in the 12th conjunct Sun and Venus. Rodney's severe beating by the police in 1991 was the trigger for the very intense race riots in Los Angeles. Pim Fortuyn, after whose murder violent riots broke out on the Binnenhof, once told in an interview that a woman had predicted a violent death for him. He had Patrocles-Menoetius in the 12th house opposite 148975 2001 XA255 *(rejection-acceptance issues)*; square Pholus/1993 SB/Viv/ Principia *(sudden destruction of life due to upheld principle)*; square Thereus/ Dong *(Fortuyn was not sexually blackmailable)*; trine Rhadamanthus *(strong sense of carrying out justice)*. Martin Luther King had Patrocles-Menoetius, among other things, conjunct 2002 TC302 *(obsession with politics, stressful conditions)* and Nike *(victory)*; sextile Chiron/Klytaemnestra *(showing a blind spot with a deadly wound)*; opposite Pandora *(airing dirty laundry)*. The for his provocatively expressed freedom of speech or film about Fortuyn's murder, murdered Theo van Gogh, had Patrocles-Menoetius sextile Ascendant; trine Typhon *(fighting)*; square Heracles/Nemesis/North Lunar Node *(harsh judgment, forcefully expressed, fate execution)*; square Moons *(personality)*. In a positive aspect, if controlled, Patrocles-Menoetius can provide an empowerment of useful aspects, as well as technical and strategic aptitude. This Trojan does not stimulate the imagination and operates initially in an offensive or aggressive manner. However, it has a flip side. In the discovery chart, the Sun is conjunct Crantor *(sudden death but also realizing the tenderness and vulnerability of life)*. Patrocles-Menoetius itself is trine Chiron *(wounded healer, showing a blind spot)* and trine 2002 VR128 *(deeply human spirituality)*. Forensically: talented ballet or dance coaches and trainers at a professional level.

The orbital period is 11 years and 336 days.

4543 PHOINIX
Regeneration, physical and/or mental rebirth

L4-Trojan discovered by Carolyn Shoemaker on February 2, 1989, with a diameter of 62.79 km. Phoinix, from the Greek φοίνιξ (phóinix), was long associated with Phoenician, date palm, or purple. However, Greek mythology knew the legendary bird Phoinix, which aged significantly, then burst into flames, only to be reborn from its own ashes.

The interpretation of Phoinix in the horoscope suggests regeneration, physical and/or mental rebirth, typically related to fire-related issues such as burnout or a mental shift in anger management. Particularly favorable outcomes can arise with a trine or conjunction of Phoinix to Mars, Jupiter, Sun, or Ascendant, especially in the recovery from burnout. Of note is the position of the regeneration planet Pluto at 15 degrees and 7 arcminutes of Scorpio, just a few arcminutes from the exact location where Via Combusta, the Burned Way, ends. Additionally, it is close to the corrected Black Moon in the 30th degree of Virgo, the sign of health recovery and taking care of one's body.

At the time of discovery, Phoinix itself was positioned in the 8th degree of Leo under the influence of the Mars-Sun-like star Asellus Australis, conjunct AMOS, and trine Hygeia. Forensically, Phoinix primarily refers to individuals who had experienced burnout but have since recovered or are in the process of recovering.

The orbital period is 11 years, 186 days, and 12 hours.

13062 PODARKES

An urge to score, coupled with a somewhat petty inclination to prove oneself at the last moment, leading to mishaps and conflicts, particularly in the realm of relationships and sexuality; conflicts; negative change of mood after drugs or alcohol; sprinters; men defeated by women

Podarkes, a medium-sized L4 Jupiter Trojan from the Greek camp, has a diameter of about 29 kilometers (later estimated 40 km. in 2018). Podarkes was discovered on April 19, 1991 by the American astronomer couple Carolyn and Eugene Shoemaker at the Palomar Observatory in California. It was identified as the main entity of the proposed Podarkes family and takes its name from the figure Podarkes or Podarces from Greek mythology. The orbit of this Trojan asteroid is thought to be unstable. It is located in the anterior Lagrangian point of Jupiter (L4) within the Greek camp, 60° ahead of its orbit., corresponding to, with a semimajor axis of 5.16 AU.

In Greek mythology, *Podarces*, Ποδάρκης in Ancient Greek, was the descendant of Iphiclus, descendant of Phylacus, the founder of Phylace, and Diomedeia. A brother of Protesilaus, they are alternately labeled in various accounts as the sons of Phylacus and Astyoche. In Homer's Iliad, Podarces and Protesilaus are represented as former suitors of Helena. Honorably, they defended the marital rights of Menelaus, Helen's husband, when the latter was kidnapped by Paris. After the death of Protesilaus at the hands of Hector, Podarces took charge of the Phylacian forces in the Trojan War and sided with the Greeks. The Posthomerica of Quintus of Smyrna tells of his downfall at the hands of Penthesilea, the formidable queen of the Amazons.

Podarkes (literally: Swift-footed) was retrograde at the time of discovery in the 20th degree of Libra, conjunct Rhiponos *(man-mouse issues)* in Libra, positioned opposite the discovery Sun in the 29th degree of Aries. The Sun formed a square aspect with Amycus *(power urge, abuse of power)*. Mars, located in Cancer, squared Neoptolemus *(initiation of conflict)* in Libra and squared Alicanto *(golden light, phoenix, self-regeneration)*. Mercury, situated in 220 Aries, was conjunct 1996 TL66 *(eruption)*/Schutz/Unruh/Vicars/Dionysus/Alu, opposing Pyrrhus, and forming a trine with Randi in Leo and Toro/Eros in Sagittarius. Saturn in 7 Aquarius was positioned on 1999 RA215 *(attacks)* and 2000 BL41 *(abundance)*. Neptune in Capricorn was on 1999 TD10 *(invasion)*, at the midpoint of Damocles in Libra and Eris in Aries from two squares.

Podarkes embodies an energy marked by a strong dissonance between the desire for swift action and the tangible realization of goals. There is a pronounced Aries-like urge to score, coupled with a somewhat petty inclination to prove oneself at the last moment, leading to mishaps and conflicts, particularly in the realm of relationships and sexuality. Power conflicts are not tolerated in advance, yet their projection can paradoxically invoke them. Ingesting drugs or alcohol heightens the risk of a foul mood or a bad trip or getting infected by a negative entity. Thoughts are often sexually inclined and there can be a fondness for erotic literature. This energy can only become constructive when the impulsiveness, tendency towards assertive behavior, and emotional outbursts are overcome, and the fire is controlled (North Lunar Node in Capricorn), purging the negative traits of Sagittarius. Then, this Trojan can excel in substantial and stable productivity, contributing to the overall indications of the individual's horoscope. The position of Podarkes in the discovery chart, opposite the sign of the Sun, suggests that despite inherent mental-emotional chaos, there is considerable ambition present that can ultimately tame and cultivate this energy.

Forensically, Podarkes indicates individuals who are quick, runners, sprinters, people in a hurry; aggrieved troublemakers or irritable individuals who are called to order; men with big mouths who may be submissive to their wives or, in extreme cases, meet their demise (literally or figuratively) at the hands of a woman; aggressive or self destructive drunkards; people possessed by an evil entity after the use of drugs or alcohol.

The orbital period is 11 years and 265 days.

4708 POLYDOROS

Manifesting multitalent through cultivating patience; experiencing a profound love for the life partner or beloved approaching the spiritual; aversion to mass culture

L5 Trojan discovered on September 11, 1988, by Carolyn Shoemaker. The interpretation leans towards possessing many qualities, talents, and abilities on various levels. Behind this lies an extremely perceptive nature that seeks artistic or philosophical expression. Other characteristics include a very quick mind; the ability to feel through the beloved, perceiving the totality of their human limitations and vulnerabilities, and experiencing a profound love for the person bordering on the spiritual. The pitfall for Polydoros is the tendency to want too much, too quickly, driven by overconfidence and self-overestimation.

Balancing through a tempering planet or another celestial body is useful to prevent the squandering of talents. If Polydoros stands strong, for example, with a significant aspect to the Sun, Moon, MC, or Ascendant, there is a risk of wasting and ruining much in life due to an underlying tendency towards impatience or anger at the mediocrity of the masses and mass culture. Polydoros might be one of the most impatient forces within the astrological arsenal. It can pose a challenging factor in the charts of highly gifted children, but on the other hand, it can lead late bloomers to magnificent flourishing when they can finally converge and manifest all their talents towards achievable goals. Opposed to Polydoros' problematic impatience is a stimulus for the development of lateral intelligence that is well above average. Forensically, it may be associated with the sudden loss of a loved one.

The orbital period is 12 years and 58 days.

5283 PYRRHUS

Emotional wildfire ignited by repression, unstoppable once lit; a desire to destroy a deceitful, disturbed government or regime; intense aversion to power built on lies rather than authority; tendencies towards violence; applying a form of scorched earth to restore natural order; fascination with fire or arson; the urge to triumph; stoking the 'fire' beneath something, animating or revitalizing it

Discovered on January 31, 1986, by Carolyn Shoemaker, Pyrrhus boasts a diameter of 82 km. This is an immensely intense energy, fiery to the core. At lower levels or in a child or adolescent's natal chart, a more than healthy fascination with fire and arson might manifest, potentially associating Pyrrhus with pyromania or forensically linking it to arson. (Of interest to insurers, especially in conjunction with Vesta and financial players like Midas, Rockefellia, or 1998 BU48.) Pyrrhus, when strongly placed, calls for the sublimation of mental energy and emotional passion to channel its forces meaningfully.

Characteristics include emotional wildfire ignited by repression, becoming unstoppable once lit; a desire to destroy a deceitful, disturbed government or regime; intense aversion to power built on lies rather than authority; tendencies towards violence; applying a form of scorched earth to restore natural order; fascination with fire or arson, particularly an affinity for burning government buildings or structures associated with oppressive powers; the desire to triumph. In a civilized setting, Pyrrhus can provide mental superiority and significant leadership. However, in a negative horoscope, Pyrrhus can turn cruel, heartless, and destructive. This is influenced by the impact of Algenubi on this Trojan. (Discovery position in the 21st degree of Leo.)

Forensically, Pyrrhus is associated with pyromaniacs, arson, Molotov cocktails, napalm, hard-to-control fires, counter-fires started to halt wildfires. Children with a strong Pyrrhus inclination may have a keen interest in playing with fire, which can escalate significantly. Marinus van der Lubbe, manipulated by the Nazis in the Reichstag fire (a precursor to 9/11), had Pyrrhus in the 21st degree of Scorpio in the apex of a Yod (epicenter) with Thisbe in Aries *(suicide through recklessness, courage, or fire)*/ Klytia in Gemini *(self-cursing through an act with significant consequences)*; trine 1997 CR29 *(shortcut)*/Chariklo *(focus on the future)* in Pisces *(self-sacrifice)*; square TRIUMF *(triumph under crossfire)*. Marinus sought to stop the Nazis by setting fire to the Reichstag, aided by them, and was executed as a convenient scapegoat.

The orbital period is 11 years and 230 days.

188847 RHIPEUS

Exceptionally vast imagination and literary creativity; continuous inspiration, often more than one can handle; vehemently opposed to black-and-white thinking in masses or groups; a human ethics dissonant with the ethics of 'the plan of the cosmos/God/gods', etc., with flaws in humanity sharply perceived

L5 Trojan discovered on March 23, 2006, by Calvin College. Rhipeus, known during the Trojan War as the most just man among all Trojans, received no recognition from the gods for his virtue. Rhipeus bestows an exceptionally vast imagination and literary creativity, bringing continuous inspiration, often more than one can handle. It intensifies opposition to black-and-white thinking in masses or groups, raising awareness of children's rights and the rights of the vulnerable. Strongly positioned in the chart this Trojan fosters a critical perspective regarding widely accepted societal norms that are inherently unjust or inhumane, persisting as blind spots, whether these issues are addressed or not. Rhipeus challenges cultural thought patterns and incorrect conceptions related to the idea of karma, God's will, etc. Moreover, there may be a connection with beloved individuals who pass away before their time. Mark Andrew Holmes associates Rhipeus, among other things, with recognizing goodness regardless of the situation and the absence of a 'why' for some events or experiences.

The orbital period is 11 years and 311 days.

3391 SINON

A nexus of pain, deceit, and neuroses; a perpetual sense of unrest accompanied by an obsessive focus on intricate details; a media-manipulator, or in contrast, an astute analyst deciphering the simulated reality crafted by media manipulations, advertisements, and compromised journalism; an innate yearning for psycho-synthesis and finding a soul-mate; a release of tension sought through the realms of sex and eroticism

Sinon, designated as 3391 Sinon, is a mid-sized L4 Jupiter Trojan positioned in the Greek camp, boasting an estimated diameter of about 40 kilometers (25 miles). This celestial body was first identified on 18 February 1977 by Japanese astronomers Hiroki Kosai and Kiichirō Furukawa at the Kiso Observatory in Japan. Sinon, a dark Jovian asteroid, exhibits a rotation period of 8.1 hours, likely featuring an elongated shape.

Its nomenclature is derived from the Greek hero Sinon of mythological lore. In the narratives of Greek mythology, Sinon (Ancient Greek: Σίνων, originating from the verb 'σίνομαι'—sinomai, meaning 'to harm, to hurt') or Sinopos emerges as a notable figure during the Trojan War. While absent in Homer's accounts, his tale unfolds in Virgil's Aeneid and other sources, portraying Sinon as a deceitful agent of the Greeks. His infamous role involves misleading the Trojans and persuading them to usher the Trojan Horse into their city, a pivotal event in the war's outcome. Depictions of Sinon in various artworks often depict him being led into Troy as a captive, with the Trojan Horse looming ominously in the background.

Someone with a dominant influence of Sinon in the horoscope will experience immense unrest and is prone to the development of neuroses. There is an obsession with details, akin to an afflicted Sun or Mercury in Virgo, the sign where Sinon fills the first degree in the discovery chart. Alongside the inner mental turmoil, there is simultaneously such a strong need to relax through sex and erotica that the individual may perceive their own character as schizoid. A strong but afflicted Sinon may create a media manipulator or political indoctrinator.

Balance is the path to alleviate this tense disposition, as indicated by the North Nodes in Libra. Sinon has a strong Uranian influence and can flood someone's mind with ideas, leading to the stagnation of these ideas after failed attempts to achieve the desired psychosynthesis that a person with a dominant Sinon longs for. It is advisable for this individual to learn to pierce through the simulated reality pushed upon us by the mass media, and clearly distinguish it from the real, human, and natural reality. By rejecting false collective assumptions, indoctrination, and certainties (Black Moons in Gemini and Taurus), this person can find their own stable core and become the master of the many contrasting qualities of Sinon. Such an individual can become a masterfully sharp analyst of media manipulations, advertisements, bribed journalists and media, etc. (Mars conjunct Manwë-Thorondor). There is a high ambition drive that only finds fitting expression when the 'ghost in the machine' (the consciousness of consciousness) is sufficiently developed. Additionally, there is a very strong desire for a soulmate.

Forensically, Sinon may indicate pain or deceit; complex processes where projects stall on certain details that one wants to clarify first; societal disillusionment regarding the simulated reality; advertising blunders and failed PR campaigns; one-night stands; blackouts of electrical networks due to overload via transmission towers and/or charging point for electrical vehicles; communication network failures, and damaged roads and railways due to earthquakes, floods, or nuclear disasters. However, multiple strong indicators in the momentary chart are required for the latter.

The orbital period is 12 years and 78 days.

15913 TELEMACHUS

Engaging from a distance; internet polemics; satellite espionage; overwhelming situations; something one fights against and will likely eventually conquer, but is currently too large, strong, or elusive; fluctuating vigilant thoughts

L4 Trojan, discovered on October 1, 1997, by the Uppsala-DLR Trojan Survey. The name Telemachus, the son of Odysseus, means distant warrior or fighter from the Greek *tēle mákomai* (τῆλε μάχομαι), *têlémachos* (τηλέμαχος). Characteristics include all forms of conflict or fighting against something without direct confrontation but involving a form of distance. This encompasses many writers of articles and investigative journalistic books, as well as satellite espionage, HAARP actions, military resonance experiments on targets, drone pilots, (hypothetical) long-range missiles, etc.

On a psychological level, there are recurring cycles of revenge thoughts that diminish and return cyclically but always simmer somewhere in the back of the mind. It involves operating in service to transform into autonomous servitude, unlearning pettiness, overly analytical perspectives, neurotic behavior, and subservience; learning to consciously grasp the big picture alongside the details. A unique aspect of Telemachus is the strength and endurance that ultimately conquers the enemy or obstacle against all expectations and despite everyone being convinced it would never succeed. Forensically: sleeper cells; unexpected and unpredictable attacks that have a significant impact; abrupt or highly original takeovers or exercises of power.

The orbital period is 11 years and 321 days.

2797 TEUCER

Uranian energie but also a dreamy, feminine, and romantic nature; experiencing disillusionment in passionate desires and feeling cursed in them, projecting inner anger onto the 'system' or circumstances, recurring tendencies towards depression

Teucer stands as a sizable Jupiter Trojan located in the L4 Lagrangian point, orbiting ahead of Jupiter in the Greek camp. This dark D-type asteroid, measuring approximately 110 kilometers in diameter, was discovered on June 4, 1981, by American astronomer Edward Bowell at the Anderson Mesa Station near Flagstaff, Arizona. A member of the 20 largest Jupiter Trojans, Teucer possesses a rotation period of 10.15 hours. It draws its name from the famed Greek hero and accomplished archer, Teucer.

In the annals of the Trojan War, Teucer distinguished himself as a skilled archer, launching arrows from behind the formidable shield of his half-brother, Ajax the Great. Despite his prowess, his attempts to shoot Hector were repeatedly thwarted by Apollo, the Trojan protector. Teucer's valor was evident in the number of Trojans he vanquished, including Hector's charioteer, Archeptolemus. Notably, after Ajax's demise, Teucer valiantly guarded his half-brother's body against opposition from Menelaus and Agamemnon. In a tragic turn, Teucer faced trial and disownment by his father after Ajax's suicide, accused of negligence for not bringing Ajax's body and arms back. Banished from Salamis Island, he set out to find a new home. His departure was marked by memorable words captured in Horace's Odes, urging companions not to despair and forecasting future voyages. Teucer's journey led him to join King Belus of Tyre in a campaign against Cyprus, culminating in the establishment of the city of Salamis on the island. His marriage to Eune, daughter of Cinyras, brought forth a daughter named Asteria.

The name Teucer carries connections to the West Hittite God Tarku (East Hittite Teshub), the Indo-European Storm God, elucidating his ties to Belus, associated with the Carthaginian god Baal Hammon. Intriguingly, local legends in Pontevedra, Galicia, claim ties to Teucer, potentially influenced by ancient Greek traders, earning the city poetic monikers like 'The City of Teucer,' with its inhabitants being referred to as teucrinos. Numerous sporting clubs in the municipality also pay homage to Teucer in their names.

Teucer possesses a more dreamy, feminine, and romantic nature, yet, at the same time, exhibits a distinctly Uranian character. Characteristics include a desire to explore the boundaries of perception and mindsets, experiencing disillusionment in passionate desires and feeling cursed in them, projecting inner anger onto the 'system' or circumstances, recurring tendencies towards depression, a penchant for an all-or-nothing approach in relationships with high expectations, and dreams of a glorious career as an artist, photographer, filmmaker, or musician. Occasionally someone with a dominant Teucer has an abrupt urge to do something about their situation as otherwise 'it will be too late'.

Forensically Teucer can represent the lonely dreamy romantic and sad and lonely but rich figure in a materially well established family. Those unlucky in love. Decadent dreamers.

The orbital period is 11 years and 195 days.

4834 THOAS

Impatience, frustrations with delays; an understanding and vision far ahead of consensus; hasty remarks, theories, conclusions, writings, or decisions; accelerating the pace

L4 Trojan with a diameter of 86.82 km, discovered on January 11, 1989, by Carolyn Shoemaker. The name Thoas has various origins in Greek mythology and is derived from θοάζω (thoazo), which can be translated as *moving quickly, advancing rapidly, running hard.*

In Thoas, the deformation of yang energy is linked to speed. Thoas comes into its own when, if strongly placed, one can learn to handle patience. This means organizing life in a way that doesn't continually frustrate this patience, especially if the overall chart is dynamic, fiery, and vital. Avoiding a 9 to 5 job where time is simply passed on a work island is crucial. In an intellectually or strongly Uranus-influenced chart, Thoas has very little patience with many things. Everything seems too slow, especially when listening to others' stories. Thoas can learn to cope with this, but some situations, influenced mainly by the house and sign Thoas occupies, remain challenging.

Characteristics: impatience, frustrations with delays; an understanding and vision far ahead of consensus; hasty remarks, theories, conclusions, writings, or decisions; accelerating the pace. Thoas is influenced by Kochab (former pole star) and Acubens (skittish nature) in the 14th degree of Leo. Forensically, Thoas is associated with all things or processes where Russia takes a lead over the rest of the world.

The orbital period is 11 years and 361 days.

9799 THRONIUM
Sexual liberation or emancipation; emotional strength, libido and creativity; diplomatic skills that are suddenly put to an end or terminated by the authorities; investigative journalism

Thronium, provisional name: 1996 RJ, is a large L4 Jupiter Trojan from the Greek camp and the parent body of a small, unnamed asteroid family (006), about 68 kilometers in diameter. It was discovered on Sept. 8, 1996, by American astronomer Timothy Spahr at the Catalina Station of the Steward Observatory near Tucson, Arizona, in the United States. The putative C-type asteroid is among the 50 largest Jupiter Trojans and has a relatively long rotation period of 21.52 hours. It is named after the ancient Greek city Thronium mentioned in the Iliad.

Thronium or Thronion (Ancient Greek: Θρόνιον) was a significant ancient Greek town, serving as the principal settlement of the Locrians, an ancient Greek tribe that inhabited the region of Locris in Central Greece, around Parnassus. Positioned 20 *stadia* (20 x 600 Greek feet approximately 3,5 - 4 km) from the coast and 30 stadia from Scarpheia, it stood alongside the Boagrius River, described by Strabo as intermittently dry and, at times, flowing with a stream. Homer mentions Thronium in the Catalogue of Ships in the Iliad, placing it in proximity to the river Boagrius. During the onset of the Peloponnesian War in 431 BCE, Thronium fell under Athenian control. In 426 BCE, an earthquake partially destroyed the town. Subsequently, in the Third Sacred War, Onomarchus, the Phocian general, captured Thronium, selling its inhabitants into slavery.

Based on the discovery-chart, a strongly positioned Thronium will result in all kinds of affinities with sex, sexual liberation, sexual emancipation and diplomacy. Such an individual can even achieve significant prominence within this field, as there is considerable ambition in this regard. However, this activity can also end in repression or sudden termination. This is indicated by the discovery position of Thronium opposing the discovery-Sun in relation to: Sun conjunct Zhulong *(diplomacy)*/1988 XB*(sex)*/Crantor *(sudden death or termination)* sextile Arrakoth *(need for attention, exposure, false reality)*; trine 1998 WW24/1998 WU31 *(power politics)*; opposition Phoinix *(rebirth)* in the sex degree 17 Pisces. Also playing a role are: 2005 PQ21 *(strong preoccupation with sex and a strong sex drive)* conjunct Bienor *(fame one has worked for)* in Aquarius *(stretch borders, break the consensus)*. Venus in 2 Leo conjunct Mars in the anaretic degree of Leo *(increased libido, an almost neurotic creative drive)*. Venus opposition Uranus and trine Pluto/Quaoar *(pornography, creative or artistic pornography, abnormally large creativity/artisticity, sexual open-mindedness, preferably developing these things organically within a wiki-like growth structure if communicative)*. Mercury in Libra conjunct Pholus and Itokawa tends towards investigative journalism or communicatively addressing issues within the aforementioned themes. Neptune in Capricorn is opposed to Sila-Nunam *(masturbation, flow)* sextile Eris *(never give up, aggression, engaging in conflict)*. Mars in Cancer is trine 1994 JS in Scorpio *(tremendous strength)*. The North Nodes are in Libra. The discovery position of Thronium in 12 Pisces conjunct 1995 QY9 *(passion)* makes a strong trine with Chrisodom *(anal sex, wit, sharp mind)* in Cancer.

Madonna has Thronium in 26 Sagittarius conjunct Galactic Center *(shedding old identities and stepping into our authentic selves)* /Narcissus *(self-centeredness)* /Hidalgo *(walking over ice-floes)* /Kassandra *(personalized language, miscommunication)* /2000 OM67; trine 1998 HK151 *(propaganda, NLP)* and sextile Jupiter/North Node *(expansion, money, contacts, current incarnation fate)*.

Forensically, Thronium can refer to a throne or a symbolic throne position *(monopoly)*, a city that perished, as well as denoting anal sex as part of passionate expression in both a male and female chart.

The orbital period is 11 years and 302 days.

20952 TYDEUS

Mastering multitasking versus chronic stress from being constantly engaged on two or more fronts; exhaustion from attention scattering; tidal flows, both literally and figuratively in the form of recurring cycles; bookkeeping/budget monitoring

L4 Trojan Tydeus was discovered on September 25, 1973, by Johannes van Houten, Ingrid van Houten-Groeneveld, and Tom Gehrels. The name Tydeus likely comes from Aeolic Greek and is derived from τύδαι (tudai) or (tydai), meaning *here* or *there*. Tydeus was the name of an Aeolic hero from the myth of the Seven Against Thebes. Characteristics: practical organizational talents; serious; responsible; mastering multitasking versus chronic stress from being constantly engaged on two or more fronts; exhaustion from attention scattering; tidal flows, both literally and figuratively in the form of recurring cycles; bookkeeping/budget monitoring. With afflictions, there is a risk of stress-related issues, intestinal or prostate problems. Affection is expressed more through actions than words. Maintaining a sense of humor and openness on an emotional level are important for inner balance and may need extra development. The deformation of yang energy in Tydeus lies in going overboard with this energy, so caution is needed through planning and self-made organizational skills.

The orbital period is 11 years and 315 days.

VENUS CO-ORBITALS

524522 ZOOZVE

Pulsating energy that is triggered to show the worst alter ego of Eris (never ending strife), lies, fake-news by mainstream media or sexual frustration; a deeper urge to solve a conflict or injustice by creating intelligent new perspectives

524522 Zoozve (provisional designation 2002 VE68) is a temporary co-orbital and quasi-satellite of planet Venus, making it the first object of its kind discovered around a major planet in the Solar System. The other three Venus co-orbitals are (322756) 2001 CK32, 2013 ND15, and 2012 XE133 of which 2013 ND15 is the only classical trojan (who at the time of this writing has not et received a PC-number. With a nearly identical orbital period around the Sun as Venus, Zoozve seemingly orbits Venus in a frame of reference rotating with the planet, completing one Venerean year. However, it primarily orbits the Sun, not Venus. Zoozve was discovered on November 11, 2002, by Brian A. Skiff at Lowell Observatory. Spectrally identified as an X-type asteroid with an assumed albedo of 0.25, Zoozve has an estimated diameter of 236 meters, a rotational period of 13.5 hours, and a light curve suggesting a potentially elongated or contact binary body.

Identified as a quasi-satellite of Venus in 2004, Zoozve exhibits resonant behavior with Venus, Mercury, and Earth. Co-orbital with Venus for approximately the last 7,000 years, it is projected to be ejected from this arrangement around 500 years from now. Despite its proximity to Earth, numerical simulations suggest that an actual collision within the next 10,000 years is unlikely. However, its frequent close approaches within 0.05 AU of Earth, with periodicity every 8 years due to its near 8:13 resonance with Earth, classify Zoozve as a Potentially Hazardous Asteroid (PHA). The asteroid experienced a close encounter on November 7, 2010, approaching Earth within 0.035 AU, and another fly-by occurred on November 4, 2018, at 0.038 AU.

The asteroid received its numerical designation from the Minor Planet Center on May 18, 2019 (M.P.C. 114620). On January 26, 2024, an episode dedicated to this asteroid was broadcast on the Radiolab podcast. Co-host Latif Nasser first encountered the asteroid's name, 'ZOOZVE', on his child's solar system poster. The name originated from a misreading by artist Alex Foster, who misinterpreted the asteroid's provisional designation '2002VE'. Brian A. Skiff subsequently proposed the name 'Zoozve' to the International Astronomical Union's Working Group Small Bodies Nomenclature (WGSBN) on behalf of

Nasser. The WGSBN approved and officially announced the name on February 5, 2024.

Astrologically Zoozve is a very complex but intriguing object. It points at an ongoing, oscillating desire, at times simmering and at times pulsating towards eruption, to set things right, even if it means resorting to extreme violence—yet not acting upon it due to the awareness of placing oneself in the position of the baby being thrown out with the bathwater. Inclined towards highly dogmatic thinking within a rebellious or revolutionary connotation. Tenacious; Scorpio-Aquarius energy accumulating in Eris *(fighting to the end, never giving up)* as a result of Eris's position in the discovery chart in Aries at the apex (epicenter) of an exact Yod formed with the Sun in Scorpio and Makemake *(peak performance)* in Virgo. This is further enhanced by the extremist tendencies of a Uranus-Orcus opposition. When the state of passive smothering of Zoozve energy within the overall context of the horoscope evolves to a higher level, emerging from the realization that engaging in a battle prematurely would be too intense and lead to self-destruction (Mars conjunct Dziewanna square Nessus), a higher spiritual and strongly Venusian insight initiates a new direction of thought. This has a much better chance of leading to something constructive and possibly a valuable transition concept. However, Zoozve continues to grapple with its impulsive core (discovery position in 24 Aries conjunct 2001 SQ73/1996 TP66, a total allergy to liars and promise breakers and the will to expose them and condemn them, emerging in unpredictable pulses). This asteroid has a suppressive effect on sexual self-expression. The libido is intensified but has almost no outlet, creating an additional source for Eris-like tendencies towards strife.

Due to its very short orbital period this asteroid is only interesting when in a fixated or almost fixated position (birth chart, progressed chart, solar or lunar return chart) as a transit will be weak in effect.

The orbital period is 225 days.

322756 2001 CK32

Distortion in every way; deep inner conflicts projected aggressively onto the outside world by means of manipulation; infighting; every obstacle is perceived as an attack on personal freedom and reacted to harshly; criminally or politically inclined

2001 CK32 is a small near-Earth object of the Aten group, measuring 0.8 km in diameter that was discovered by LINEAR on Februari 13, 2001. It is also a transient Venus co-orbital, and a Mercury grazer as well as an Earth crosser. It was once designated as a potentially hazardous asteroid.

The discovery chart of 2001 CK32 is of a rare kind that hardly leaves any room for positive qualities. There is an intrinsic mix of aggression, frustration, and an inner, panic-driven eagerness to fight one's way in, while there is a dissonance between one's inner feelings and thinking and what one says to believe. No integrity, just a distorted mix of heavy influences ending in useless manipulations, which may appear successful to the outside world but result in nothing but inner desolation.

Forensically, 2001 CK32 may indicate a politician who commits suicide, a femme fatale who ends up bankrupt or dead, or a narcissistic propaganda or media specialist who ends up – so to speak – like a Joseph Goebbels.

The orbital period is 225 days and 16 hours.

MARS TROJANS

5261 EUREKA

The resolution of a problem, a profound insight that has long been awaited, making an invention or discovery, conducting research, seeing light in the darkness

L5-Mars Trojan discovered on June 20, 1990, by David H. Levy and Henry Holt. Named after the Greek "Heureka" ("I have found it!"). The exclamation became famous as Archimedes reportedly shouted "eureka" loudly while running naked through the streets of Syracuse, having discovered the Archimedean principle in his bath. Since then, "eureka" has become a joyful cry when someone has solved a difficult problem.

Eureka is estimated to measure 2 to 4 km. The interpretation indeed suggests the resolution of a problem, a profound insight that has been long-awaited, making an invention or discovery, seeing light in the darkness, or the successful completion of a long process or quest. Aspects by important transiting planets or objects to Eureka in the natal or progressed chart are the activators of 'Eureka-moments'. A conjunction with Chiron (blind spot, wound in the soul), preferably, is the most significant.

The orbital period is 1 year and 322 days.

101429 1998 VF31

Rapidly integrating into something; young super talent; quickly reaching the highest ranks of a professional niche, a turbo career that breaks down early due to gaps in personal development, making the status suddenly feel undesired

L5-Mars Trojan, discovered on November 13, 1998, by LINEAR. Characteristics of 1998 VF31 include rapidly integrating into something; young super talent; quickly reaching the highest ranks of a professional niche, a turbo career that breaks down early due to gaps in personal development, making the status suddenly feel undesired. 1998 VF31 is associated with the entire psychological developmental issues faced by gifted children, such as gaining admiration for their talent when what they need is love and normal affection, crucial in upbringing. A child may feel relegated to a cold pedestal swamped with parental pride, missing a genuine childhood for the rest of their lives. Later in life, there's an irresistible urge to radically change personal life. Often, there's a simultaneous very drastic career change, or one sheds the burden and curse of status through drugs, music, or embarking on a spiritual path. Holding a strongly aspected and positioned 1998 VF31 somewhere, one lives a life feeling on the border of two worlds, times, or realities. Forensic: the prodigy; people reaching the top in something in their early twenties or late teens.

The orbital period is 1 year and 321 days.

311999 2007 NS2

Very critical stance; troublemaker with a sharp tongue; entering, saving, or breaking off a relationship, contract, or collaboration at the last moment; learning to handle freedom and idealism in a more sympathetic and less demanding way

L5-Mars Trojan, discovered on July 14, 2007, by the Observatorio Astronómico de La Sagra in Andalusia. 2007 NS2 was in the 12th degree of Aquarius conjunct the star Armus *(Mars/Mercury-like sharp, critical, shameless, troublesome)* and Scylla *(the critical note)*; opposition Utopia/Hecate; square Amycus; trine Messalina.

Very critical stance; troublemaker with a sharp tongue; entering, saving, or breaking off a relationship, contract, or collaboration at the last moment; learning to handle freedom and idealism in a more sympathetic way; remarkable and deep psychic and mystical insights that occur abruptly or unexpectedly or under unusual circumstances. Characteristic of the dominant pattern of a 2007 NS2 is that of someone who, at some point (usually in midlife), loses their wild hairs, becomes a lot less egocentric, and a much more likable person than before. Usually, a profound psychic or mystical experience precedes this with a turning point effect. Forensic: fierce critics who come across as unguided projectiles.

The orbital period is 1 year and 322 days.

385250 2001 DH47

A brilliant and accurate sense of humor in all forms; rich imagination linked to humor or absurdistic representations; problems with career choice; escaping tricky situations by simply transcending them

L5-Mars Trojan discovered on February 20, 2001, by Spacewatch. 2001 DH47 measures 562 meters in diameter. Everything revolves around humor for this Mars Trojan. Characteristics: a brilliant and accurate sense of humor in all forms; rich imagination linked to humor or absurd representations; intelligent and empathetic regarding humor; problems with career choice; making meaningless orientation trips regarding career choice; escaping tricky situations by simply transcending them; humor as a survival mechanism; preference for British humor. Forensic: comedians; British humor.

The orbital period is 1 year and 322 days.

121514 1999 UJ7
Detecting flaws and unsupported assumptions within the scientific, religious, or spiritual consensus

Currently te only L4-Mars Trojan. It has a diameter of 1 km, and was discovered on October 30, 1999, by LINEAR. Characteristics include detecting flaws in scientific developments and growing systems; exposing the Achilles' heel in scientific assumptions and axioms; seeing through and criticizing complex scientific mind frames set as consensus; 'heresy', undermining beliefs; exposing flaws and absurdities in religious or spiritual mind frames; interests in the paranormal and independent science.

The orbital period is 1 year and 322 days.

URANUS TROJAN

636872 2014 YX49

Sensitive and mediumistic; protective instinct; highly sexually engaged; expressing criticism of 'the normal'; affinity with the twilight, the dark, the classical underworld; sharp and witty mind

2014 YX49 is a centaur and a Uranus co-orbital, with an approximate diameter of 77 kilometers, first identified on December 26, 2014, through the Pan-STARRS survey. Notably, it is the second confirmed centaur on a tadpole orbit with Uranus and the fourth Uranus co-orbital discovered, following 83982 Crantor, 2011 QF99, and (472651) 2015 DB216. In terms of its characteristics, Centaur 2014 YX49 functions as a temporary L4 Trojan of Uranus, the second to be confirmed in such a resonant state after 2011 QF99. Its presence as an L4 Uranian Trojan is estimated to have persisted for around 60,000 years, and it has the potential to maintain this state for an additional 80,000 years. Numerical integrations indicate the possibility of its continuous residence within Uranus' co-orbital zone for nearly one million years. 2014 YX49 is also entrapped in the 7:20 mean motion resonance with Saturn. Interestingly, this resonant configuration is shared with the other known Uranian Trojan, 2011 QF99. This was the first known Uranus Trojan to be discovered. However so far it lacks a MPC-number.

Keywords: sensitive and mediumistic; protective instinct; highly sexually engaged, but with a tendency towards anxiety regarding sexual expression; the fusion of the sexual with the occult, the entirely different, or magical linked to the fear of being destroyed by the twisted norm of the status quo; expressing criticism of 'the normal' by undermining that which normalizes itself; Luciferian intense energy; vitalism; Promethean; a mystical and sensitive affinity with the twilight, the dark, the classical underworld, and the depths or dark recesses of the soul; love for truth, even when uncomfortable; feeling threatened by the System (political, religious, or other corporate variants) or undergoing an invasion of the System with harmful impact; being the opponent against one's will and from self-integrity having no other choice; great physical and mental strength, despite the sensitive nature; sharp-witted mind; a never-ending specific kind of optimism regarding one's ambition and creativity; great talent for in-depth research, investigative journalism, or other intellectual excavation; no respect for, nor patience with stupidity or institutionalized stupidity and inclined to name it hard and directly where it occurs; tendency towards revolutionary or overturning thinking; highly valuing personal freedom; collecting large amounts of knowledge and data to make this

'apocalyptic' common at a certain point; strategic intuition or, conversely, blind spots in that area; intuitively sensing that going too far in a struggle leads to one's own downfall; diplomatic ability to manipulate tactically.
Forensically 2014 YX49 may indicate the genius rebel or outcast or misunderstood but highly original artist, creative or writer; a person that can show a new horizon or frees people from their blind spot indoctrination.

The orbital period is 83 years and 245 days.

CENTAUR AND JUMPING TROJAN

316179 2010 EN65 (NAME SUGGESTION: DETONATOR)
Detonation, liberation, orgasm; effectuation

2010 EN65 has a diameter of 183 km and was discovered on March 7, 2010. This Centaur also behaves like a Jumping Trojan of Neptune, leaping from L4 to L5 via L3 (L3 is the Lagrange point that is always in opposition to the celestial body (in this case, Neptune) or L1 & L2. During extreme lightning strikes on May 28, 2016, causing dozens of injuries in Germany and France, Algol, the lightning strike star was opposite the Osc. Black Moon on the midpoint of Hexlein/2010 EN65 – set against the backdrop of Uranus/Eris opposite Typhon.

Chinese artist Cai Guo-Qiang, whose work is entirely based on detonating gunpowder, has 2010 EN65 trine Taurinensis/Lust *(strategically deployed for pleasure)*, sextile Hermes/1993 SC *(intelligently releasing something in confidence)*; sextile Varuna *(grand approach and impact in media)*; square Pavlov *(repeatedly)*. 2010 EN65 is notably dominant in the horoscopes of porn stars. After all, orgasm is a kind of detonation. Composer Richard Wagner, known for the underlying sensuality in his operas, had 2010 EN65 trine Eros.

The characteristics of this object are: detonation, trigger, effectuation, release, orgasm, complete opening, abrupt release of a lot of energy, letting go of shame or guilt, liberation, self-acceptance; also sexual drive, eroticism. The essence seems to be the stimulation of energy buildup until it needs to discharge. I suggest the name 'Detonator' for this Neptune Trojan.

The orbital period is 171 years and 229 days.

QUASI-NEPTUNE SATELLITE

309239 2007RW10

Sexual awakening; only enjoying sex after an inner fear, inhibition, or blockage has been removed; sudden turns in one's sex life that are liberating

2007 RW10 was discovered on September 9, 2007, by the Palomar Distant Solar System Survey (PDSSS) and has an approximate diameter of 247 km. This is a peculiar object. It is suspected to be a detached L5 Neptune Trojan, temporarily orbiting the Sun independently and will sooner or later jump back into the Trojan position. Characteristics include sexual awakening; being a late bloomer sexually and only letting loose later in life; enjoying sex after an inner fear, inhibition, or blockage has been removed; sudden turns in one's sex life that are liberating.

The orbital period is 166 years and 357 days.

NEPTUNE TROJANS

385695 CLETE (2005 TO74)

Ergonomics; soul ergonomics; dichotomy between pragmatism and idealism as a process that must play out; the freezing force that rising fear of the world's demise has on creativity, transcending with one's own human positive power and initiative

L4 Neptune-Trojan with a diameter of 97 km, discovered on October 8, 2005, by Scott S. Sheppard and Chad Trujillo. This Neptune Trojan was named after Clete from Greek mythology, a member of the Amazons, a fully female warrior tribe that fought on the side of the Trojans against the Greeks in the Trojan War. Clete was one of the twelve followers of the Amazon queen Penthesilea and went in search of her after she went missing during the war. According to the queen's will, Clete sailed to Italy and founded the city of Clete. The official naming citation was published by the Minor Planet Center on May 18, 2019 (M.P.C. 114955). The naming follows the scheme already established with 385571 Otrera, namely to name these Neptune Trojans after figures related to the Amazons.

The characteristics of 2005 TO74 are: ergonomic insight; last-minute negotiations or talks to save or arrange a relationship, or to maintain or break off contact with a group, or to establish or break a contract or diplomatic bond; future-oriented engagement with spirituality, water, music, film, or art; dichotomy between pragmatism and idealism, resulting in equating ideals or optimistic insights with castles in the air; drowning in a mass of spiritual information or artistic ideas and breaking or not breaking this pattern later in life. Status, worrying about details, and wanting to shine are the major hindrance to releasing the Neptunian creative potentials in 2005 TO74. There is a lot of turbidity in this energy that is only left behind when personal 'I want' is entirely clear, and a clean positive Aries energy can be displayed *(courage, pioneering, doing with an open mind, proactive)* by stripping the personal attitude of any external input, and calibrating it to self-integrity (what do you really want when there is no one suggesting what you should do).

2005 TO74 was in the 7th degree of Aries conjunct Orpheus and 1996 TO66 opposite Nyx/2003 CO1/AMOS/1988 XB at the time of discovery. In 2005 TO74, the Neptunian influence (discovery Sun/Chariklo/Ophelia/2002 GZ32) is clouded with deceitful and ugly aspects. Much of the Orpheus myth, where the brilliant musician goes to the underworld to rescue his beloved, is inherently packaged in this energy. 2005 TO74 goes through a haze of polluted Neptune energy *(lies, modified reality, false appearance, the ugliness in the world that affects the ideal)* to apply self-purification afterward from the realization that one's attitude attracts the atmosphere (Neptune) according to the nature of that attitude. You could call it a form of soul ergonomics.

Forensically, 2005 TO74 relates to: breaking patterns regarding the greenhouse effect lobby in relation to the assumption of a rising sea level. This pattern break mainly involves puncturing false propaganda (climate gate). Additional forensic characteristics are: ergonomic fitness equipment, sports ergonomics, and ergonomics related to medical equipment; camera shots, photos used to prove a partner's infidelity; movies about flood disasters; ideas about a deluge.

The orbital period is 164 years and 281 days.

385571 OTRERA (2004 UP10)

Committed spirituality; an easy fusion between imagination/ideal and willpower; imagination taking flight; great enthusiasm once the goal/soul destination is determined; focused belief; spiritual, artistic, or sexual truth-seeking; an intuitive connection with the total truth (aletheia)

L4 Neptune-Trojan Otrera has a diameter of 42 km and was discovered on October 16, 2004, by Scott S. Sheppard and Chad Trujillo in the same orbit as Neptune. Otrera is named after the first Amazon queen. With Ares, she had a daughter, Penthesilea, the Amazon queen who fought in the Trojan War. Otrera seems to hold the energy midpoint of Neptune/Moon/Aries point. As if Otrera stimulates a unity with the body it makes a conjunction with, absorbing everything and creating a kind of suction that makes the information from the conjunction's body strongly manifest from the unmanifest.

Salvador Dali had Otrera conjunct Ixion, the most interesting Plutino for his characteristic half-liquid surrealism, or the most stimulating body generally for the result he produced. Otrera, like Neptune, is watery, spiritually engaged, but more focused, although Otrera also has a clouding element due to the discovery Sun conjunct Ceto/Aten/Hybris opposite 2001 UR163. However, Otrera's strength lies in the fusion of willpower with imagination. This Trojan encourages synergy between the two and can be seen as a creative and inspiring energy. Otrera, at a higher level, has a link with an identification with the greatest of all nature spirits, Pan, in the sense that the psychic and spiritually engaged state arising from the identification with Pan magically defends against crudeness towards Mother Earth and Mother Nature and the associated nihilistic negativity. Otrera can become very persistent in this (Pluto trine Eris in the discovery chart). In addition, Otrera approaches the situation with a 'what must be must be' attitude, even if it completely disrupts the consensus to make way for something better (Neptune conjunct Damocles/Sophrosine trine Mars). There is also, like Neptune, a strong sexual dimension, where sex transitions into the mystical and covers a broad range of expression from writing erotic literature to anal sex. Otrera stimulates great fame, popularity, and media impact when the energy manifests at full strength. Otrera was in the 5th degree of Aries conjunct Veritas *(truth)* at the time of discovery, while Aletheia *(total truth)* was on the Aries point.

The orbital period is 164 years and 296 days (slightly varying orbital data are in circulation).

613490 2006 RJ103

Contact with other entities or experiencing profound spiritual insight through or during an extreme state of inner crisis; workaholic or offensive non-compromising tendencies; the capacity to renew and undergo mental and physical rebirth after a crisis or shock

2006 RJ103 was first identified by the Sloan Digital Sky Survey Collaboration at Apache Point Observatory, New Mexico, on 12 September 2006. Being the fifth discovered Neptune Trojan and the most substantial of its kind discovered, it boasts a diameter of approximately 180 kilometers. As of 2016, it maintains a distance of 30.3 astronomical units (AU) from Neptune. The observed mean diameter of 180 kilometers is derived from a magnitude of 22.0. However, employing a generic magnitude-to-diameter conversion, it is estimated to have a diameter of around 130 kilometers, utilizing an absolute magnitude of 7.5 with an assumed albedo of 0.10.

Prominent in a chart this Neptune Trojan may indicate: contact with other entities or experiencing profound spiritual insight through or during an extreme state of inner crisis; workaholic or offensive non-compromising tendencies; the capacity to renew and undergo mental and physical rebirth after a crisis or shock; belief in truth and freedom as correlated principles; fate acceptance or a critical attitude towards fate; an aggressive or warrior vibe that is dangerous or even fatal to exploit, creating a love-hate relationship with this vibe; resets of health and/or life course after self-confrontation and taking full responsibility.

In the discovery chart of 2006 RJ103, it was conjunct Eris in 21 Aries at the time of its identification. This placement formed a trine with Saturn in Leo. Additionally, there was an inconjunct aspect to its discovery-Sun/Toro in Virgo, while the Moon was positioned in Taurus in trine with the Sun/Toro conjunction. Furthermore, there was an exact square aspect to Phoinix in Capricorn. Mercury was in the anaretic 30th degree of Virgo, suggesting an inclination toward strong nerve tensions and a regular need for psycho-synthesis.

The orbital period is 163 years and 281 days.

THULE-GROUP

---

279 THULE

Transition, the afterlife, other dimensions; racism issues; UFOs, vril, orgone

279 Thule, classified as a D-type asteroid, with a diameter of 126.59 km, resides in the outer asteroid belt and is likely composed of organic-rich silicates, carbon, and anhydrous silicates. Discovered by Johann Palisa on October 25, 1888, in Vienna, Thule marked the first finding of an asteroid with a semi-major axis exceeding 4 AU. Thule became the initial member of the *Thule dynamical group*. This group, identified as of 2008, includes three objects: 279 Thule, (186024) 2001 QG207, and (185290) 2006 UB219. Their orbits, influenced by the periodic force exerted by Jupiter, are situated in the outermost edge of the asteroid belt, displaying a 4:3 orbital resonance with Jupiter, akin to the Kirkwood gaps observed in the inner regions of the asteroid belt.

Thule is named after the legendary northern island Thule, described by Pytheas in the fourth century BC as an island located six days' journey north of Great Britain. Since then, Thule became a mythical island lying at the utmost boundary of the world. The name likely originates from the proto-Indo-European term for *ground* (telu). Thule, derived from the Greek Θούλη (Thoúlē) and Latinized as Thūlē, represents the northernmost locale mentioned in ancient Greek and Roman writings as well as in cartography. The contemporary interpretations of Thule encompass regions such as Orkney, Shetland, Northern Scotland, the island of Saaremaa (Ösel) in Estonia, and the Norwegian island of Smøla. Over time, in classical and medieval literature, the term 'ultima Thule' (Latin for 'farthest Thule') took on a metaphorical sense, referring to any remote place situated beyond the 'borders of the known world'. As the Late Middle Ages and the early modern era unfolded, the Greco-Roman concept of Thule became frequently associated with the actual locations of Iceland or Greenland. At times, Ultima Thule served as a Latin designation for Greenland, particularly when Thule was used to denote Iceland.

In the horoscope, Thule indicates themes related to racial consciousness and racism, both obsession and dislike and relativity, as well as paranormal issues, particularly concerning UFOs, vril, orgone, and other phenomena falling outside mainstream scientific physics. Thule also has a connection to death, transition, the afterlife, and other dimensions. Mark Andrew Holmes further attributes intolerance or, conversely, tolerance, travel, and feelings of superiority as Thule characteristics. With a strongly aspected Thule in the natal chart, these themes play a more than average role in one's life and are periodically stirred by transits activating Thule.

The orbital period is 8 years and 307 days.

185290 2006 UB219
Political ambitions; racist and/or nationalist politics and propaganda; persecution of dissidents; desiring significant media publicity; initiating organic wiki-like networks

2006 UB219 is a Thule asteroid with a diameter of 9.5 km, discovered on October 16, 2006, by the Catalina Sky Survey in Arizona. When prominently featured in a horoscope, 2006 UB219 suggests a tendency to advocate for racist or nationalist ideas or propaganda, widespread dissemination of writings within this context, a desire to reach a large audience as a speaker or writer, a penchant for politics, fanaticism, a continual struggle between projecting confidence and an insecure, labile core, using fanaticism as an outlet for disappointment or conflicts in love, artificially suppressing inner insecurities, seeking to silence dissidents undermining one's propaganda, strong aversion to research challenging one's position, and an offensive bureaucratic or aggressive stance toward researchers or whistleblowers. It also indicates a process of discrimination or unlearning discrimination and the initiation of large organic wiki-like networks.

In historical context, 2006 UB219 was exactly conjunct the Midheaven/ Gonggong/Jabberwalk in the event-chart of Hitler's official appointment as Counselor of Germany on January 30, 11:25 local time, Berlin, symbolizing a public strive for group awareness and interaction in the face of an elusive threat, negative progression, life slipping away, and a maelstrom of fear. We have all witnessed the results. Heinrich Himmler – with Germania on his Aries-point – had 2006 UB219 within two arc minutes of an exact sextile to Orcus and in an exact semi-sextile to Pluto; square to Utopia/Varuna. Joseph Goebbels had 2006 UB219 conjunct his Descendent/Spirit/conjunct 2001 KF77 *(ring the bell to motivate)* in 20 Capricorn; sextile Eris *(strive, never give up, fanatics)*.

Forensically, it is associated with ambitious politicians in the realm of nationalism, racism, persecution of dissidents and gerontophilia.

The orbital period is 8 years and 296 days.

186024 2001 QG207

Spiritual and/or social enthusiasm, a powerful and charismatic spiritual enthusiast, significant but fluctuating popularity; standing against government lies; seeking a balance between impulsive, forceful action and tactful diplomacy

Thule asteroid of 6.9 km, discovered on August 23, 2001 by the Lowell Observatory Near-Earth-Object Search (LONEOS) at the Anderson Mesa Station in Arizona. In the discovery chart, 2001 QG207 was positioned in the third degree of Pisces, conjunct Thereus/Manwë-Thorondor; forming a trine with Hylonome/Seeberg/North Node in Scorpio; and squaring 1998 VG44. The caricature resulting from these aspects with a strongly placed 2001 QG207 is that of an impassioned, powerfully charismatic spiritual enthusiast, who garners significant but fluctuating popularity by passionately opposing government lies through their spiritual (or socially engaged) mission or preaching. There is a mix of serenity and great fear caused by the tension between standing for their own mission and the potentially dangerous backlash this provokes from authorities. Nonetheless, there is a profound trust in the 'divine power' (Sun conjunct Thekla/Apophis square Varda/Pallas/Sethos).

In terms of mental and verbal or communicative abilities, a dominant 2001 QG207 can lead someone to excel especially within the contexts of work, sports, health(care), literature, trade, and investigation (Mercury conjunct Makemake in Virgo). This asteroid further exhibits an imbalance between projecting a tough and a gentle exterior. Inherently present is both the option to work as a smooth operator with the necessary tact and the option to swiftly use the blunt axe. This dichotomy is indicated by the Venus and Saturn aspecting in the discovery chart. However, the awareness that *feelings make no thinking errors* will usually prevail during these moments of friction in favor of Venus. The negative traits of Pisces *(laziness, addiction, untidiness, spiritual drifting, being out of touch with the world)* and Aquarius *(coldness, autocracy, technocracy, rebellion)* are purged and/or quickly noticed by/among others when exhibited. Forensic: the martyr, the fiery preacher or prophet, the social reformer or sect leader; the government acting as a curse.

The orbital period is 8 years and 318 days.

HILDA ASTEROIDS

8721 AMOS
Loving; social, stringent, visionary/prophetic; soul intelligence; shepherd of the flock

AMOS was discovered on January 14, 1996, measuring 49.91 km in diameter and is named after the Air Force Maui Optical Station (AMOS), which led to its discovery. However, in terms of interpretation, AMOS also has a connection with the biblical Amos and the Hebrew term for 'that which is carried.' The biblical prophet Amos became known for his involvement in economic justice and a pragmatic view of right and wrong. Prayers and sacrifices did not justify bad deeds for him, and ethical actions and doing good were more important than rituals. In his view, the Israelites were held together by a moral contract, and if everyday actions fell below a moral threshold, the people would disintegrate. Amos has always been a very popular name among Puritans.

The overlap of the psychospheric charge and historical significance associated with the name Amos in this asteroid's discovery chart is particularly noteworthy. AMOS emanates a positive, gentle, humane influence. The essence of AMOS is soul intelligence; precisely understanding what the soul is, what nourishes it, and maintaining a human balance, as well as recognizing threats or destruction to this balance and mass behavior. AMOS makes individuals highly sensitive, with the side effect of mood swings ranging from very cheerful to deep depression and vice versa.

The asteroid, if strongly placed, provides a good predisposition for developing occult abilities such as remote viewing, astro-magic, divination, and psychospheric magic. There is a strong link with water in a broad sense and authentic psychology, stripped of human techniques and the academic imbecility that currently plagues this study, consisting of ignoring the extreme pollution influences (microwave radiation, chemical pollution through food, water, and air, the mutual interference of both forms of pollution) on the human psyche. This issue is exacerbated by pressure from the rat race society and the financial system in which people live, as well as various postmodern forms of addiction such as infolapsis (pathological addiction to screen information and stimuli).

In some horoscopes, AMOS indicates talent for photography or underwater photography. Affliction may be associated with skin, respiratory, or liver problems. With a strong AMOS, it is sometimes necessary to take measures against hypersensitivity and pay extra attention to translating intuitive knowing and understanding into practical application. Others often perceive someone with a strong AMOS as angelic. This energy taps directly into a higher consciousness, as beautifully described by Anita Moorjani in her book *Dying to Be Me*, recounting her near-death experience.

The orbital period is 7 years and 273 days.

3290 AZABU

Potential for great fame or infamy, whether related to sex scandals, diplomatic blunders, or significant creative achievements or ventures; success through boldness and ambition or failure therein; achieving something through the synergy of self-discipline and one's own talent and energy

Azabu was discovered on September 19, 1973, by Cornelis Johannes van Houten, Ingrid van Houten-Groeneveld, and Tom Gehrels, measuring 24 km in diameter. Azabu is named after the observatory in Azabu, the most expensive district in Tokyo, frequented by artists, celebrities, and businessmen. The term Azabu itself means clothing of hemp.

Azabu, when prominently aspected, is an intriguing player in the realms of relationships – including diplomatic ones – love, and sex, where this context is linked to extreme or brash deeds or actions with the potential to establish enormous fame or infamy in this area. Sex scandals or incredibly tactless behavior, or at best, these themes artistically or literarily shaped, become the output. Positively, Azabu makes one capable of independently generating income streams with healthy courage and a pioneering spirit. Azabu is one of the more intense sexual asteroids, and transits (provided there is not too much interference from other celestial objects) increase libidinous needs. There is also a piece of destructive energy that one must channel effectively through creativity; otherwise, it can be self-destructive. A strong Azabu also makes individuals resistant to government interference and Orwellian intrusions, against which they can vehemently and resolutely rebel. Calibrating Saturn/Capricorn energy (North Nodes conjunct Black Moon in the 4th degree Capricorn opposite Saturn in the discovery chart) and courage (Azabu in Aries conjunct Rhiphonos in the discovery chart) is the key to turning Azabu into a positively directed force and source of inspiration. Forensically, the asteroid refers to the eponymous district in Tokyo, to hemp products, self-made millionaires in Mexico; to Israeli bully diplomacy or to successful ads or campaigns related to the theme of sleep (solutions or advice for good sleep).

The orbital period is 7 years and 338 days.

15417 BABYLON

Affinity with water; landscape and garden architecture; understanding the context and connotations of government disinformation; sexual magic; the magic and exercise of power through female sexual seduction

Babylon, discovered on February 27, 1998, by Eric Walter Ernst, carries a celestial significance associated with water, landscape, and garden architecture. At the time of discovery, it was in conjunction with the star Alkas (the cup) in the 23rd degree of Virgo, opposite Bacchus/1999 TC36/Starr; forming a trine with 1998 VG44/Els-Pizarro/Cacus; and squaring Flammario.

Key Characteristics include an affinity with water, involvement in the creation and preservation of water channels, landscape, and garden architecture. Babylon also encompasses the ability to discern the context and connotations of government disinformation, understanding the intricacies of sexual magic, and exploring the magic and exercise of power through female sexual allure. Babylon is a potent asteroid intertwining sexuality, creativity, and artistic expression, with power dynamics manifesting in sexual and religious realms. It channels a significant Piscean and Virgoan energy, with a transformative quality purging negative Virgoan traits.

This asteroid holds forensic relevance in fields such as water engineering, Delta planning, hydrocultures, landscape architecture, and historical contexts like the Hanging Gardens—the Seventh Wonder of the World. It's associated with the biblical figure, the Whore of Babylon, and the tarot card Strength/Lust, indicating themes of sexual indulgence and orgies.

The orbital period is 7 years and 316 days.

11739 BÂTON-ROUGE
A red rod, symbolism of the Ace of Rods, positive creative yang energy, potential; the place Baton Rouge

Bâton-Rouge is primarily discussed here from a forensic perspective. It is essentially a geographical asteroid with a diameter of 17 km, named after the capital of Louisiana, discovered on September 25, 1998, by amateur astronomer Walter Cooney. Bâton-Rouge can refer to a red rod, to the symbolism of the Ace of Rods, thus to positive creative yang energy, to potential, in special cases to a syringe used for blood sampling (if positioned in a 'blood degree' such as the 18th degree of Libra).

Still, its primary association is with the place Baton Rouge. Shortly after midnight on June 5, 2016, Baton Rouge witnessed a gross racially tinged police murder of 37-year-old black American Alton Sterling. Sterling was selling CDs on the street near a shopping mall, reportedly threatened several people with a gun, prompting a police call. Upon arrest and resistance by Sterling, two hefty officers pressed him to the ground. While face down, with two officers on top of him, he was senselessly shot multiple times in the heart with a gun pressed against his back. This incident was filmed and uploaded to YouTube and social media, leading to intense demonstrations and riots in various U.S. cities, including New York, where people occupied the Brooklyn Bridge, expressing their frustration with yet another incident of deadly police violence in the U.S. Sterling died at 00:46, shortly after midnight. Those who filmed and shared the incident waited to see if the police would transparently present the incident in the media, which, of course, did not happen. Instead, they disabled the material from a nearby surveillance camera.

It was a New Moon (with the Moon approaching the Sun, not Void of Course), conjunct Venus opposite Saturn, square Shadow. Bâton-Rouge was in 17 Cancer, in harsh opposition to Pluto *(intensity, transformation)*, conjunct Cyllarus *(racial riots, racism)*/Randi (here: *corporate lies*), trine Black Moon/ Nostalgia *(deep confronting awareness related to deformities in the past)*, sextile North Node *(karma)*, sextile Bienor/Aletheia/Amor/Zipfel/Spirit/Silly *(gaining great fame through truthfulness expressed sharply and with deep soul-stirring, leading to a bizarre consequence)*, square Zero/Villon/Tantalus in Aries *(a starting point related to villainous actions and tormenting from aggression)*. Silly and Randi may seem odd elements in this context, but Randi signifies not only lust but also the obscuring of truth (disabling the camera). The protests escalated to the point where snipers shot at police officers, and five were immediately killed (Silly, as too absurd for words). The two officers involved in the murder were Blane Salamoni and Howie Lake. The asteroid Verdun *(massacre)* was on the midpoint of asteroids 12780 Salamony and Bâton-Rouge, with Salomony square on houses 3 and 9 *(the axis of communication and media)* and conjunct 6 *(work, police)*, opposite 12 *(being your own enemy)*. Forensically Bâton-Rouge may denote a club or staff or red staff.

The orbital period is 7 years and 296 days.

2246 BOWELL
Crowbar, engine, great force, and stamina

Bowell was discovered on December 14, 1979, and named on January 1, 1981, after the American astronomer Edward L. G. Bowell. The asteroid measures 44.21 km in diameter. Bowell represents great diligence and work energy and, if strongly aspected, can lead to top performances in sports, research, engineering, bodybuilding, and other methods of physical perfection, technology, mechanics, and medical discoveries. Bowell is a powerhouse, but the force can be too intense and veer off course or derail itself due to a lack of nuance and emotional intelligence. The energy of Bowell is purposeful enthusiasm mixed with earthly concretization and stamina. Forensically Bowell may denote the bowels.

The orbital period is 7 years, 309 days, and 12 hours.

3254 BUS
Realizing the true course of one's life based on emotional integrity; forced relocation, transportation, or emigration

Bus was discovered on October 17, 1982, by Edward Bowell and measures 31 km in diameter. Bus is named after the American astronomer Schelte John Bus. Bus is a complex asteroid that, at the time of discovery, was in the 20th degree of Aries, conjunct the star Baten Kaitos, Machiavelli, and 1998 US43.

Characteristics include forced or compulsory transportation, being transported, emigration, or forced emigration; an accident, violent incident, a fall, or being struck by something or someone; shipwreck; rescue or being rescued. On a deeper level, Bus is ambitious and strives for a position of power but encounters problems due to a dissonance between identity and image or between personal passion and aspiration and the career goal. Bus can be an indication of trauma in the personality structure resulting from a very poor relationship with parents, where one, often forced by the situation, left the parental home too early. Personal ambitions can then easily derail into compensating for a gap or pursuing unrealistic dreams to fill a void.

Bus challenges delusions about career goals, the need to prove oneself outwardly, compensating for deficiencies, etc., and encourages individuals to abandon these ideas and map their unique will from a place of self-integrity. What do you want, and what do you not want? What is pleasant, and what is not? Answering these questions from a feeling perspective is the key. Only then can one reset their own life and create a positive flow that brings genuine inner satisfaction. Forensically, Bus refers to an autobus or storage container and bus-shaped/tubular objects.

The orbital period is 7 years and 321 days.

73769 DELPHI
Intuitively condensing contexts and connotations to their essence; predicting; bouts of sexual insatiability; sudden blossoming or collapse of personality or health

Delphi belongs to the Hilda-subcategory of the Schubart-asteroids. It was discovered on August 10, 1994, by Eric Walter Ernst and named after the famous Greek oracle where the seer Pythia delivered her predictions and advice in a trance.

Characteristics include making predictions or prognoses; the ability to intuitively condense contexts and connotations to their essence, clarifying veiled underlying processes, signals, or suspicions in oneself and others; smoothly accessing the soul, the unconscious, deep emotions; bouts of sexual insatiability, using sex to communicate what one cannot express verbally; a sudden change or complete blossoming of the personality or its collapse; a abrupt improvement or deterioration of physical health that is very dramatic.

Forensically, it refers to protests against the disturbance and torture of cetaceans with sonar and other electronic communication by the navy.

The orbital period is 7 years and 347 days.

100133 DEMOSTHENES

Reasoning, the ability to make a tremendous impact as a speaker, winning debates

Like Delphi, Demosthenes also belongs to the Hilda-subcategory of the Schubart-asteroids. It was discovered on September 15, 1993, by Eric Walter Ernst and named after the famous Greek orator of the same name. Later, he became an icon of the occult, associated with Yale University's society Skull & Bones, which incorporated his year of death, 322 BC, into their logo.

Demosthenes' influence in the natal chart mirrors the primary characteristic of the historical Demosthenes, namely, that of a brilliant orator with significant persuasive abilities. The discovery chart associates an enormous impact potential with this asteroid in this context.

The orbital period is 7 years and 296 days.

11249 ETNA

Periodic, yet unexpected eruptions; outbursts of something that has been simmering and suddenly becomes unbearable; eruptions within social media or politics; strength

Etna was discovered on March 24, 1971, by Cornelis van Houten and Ingrid van Houten-Groeneveld and named after one of the most active volcanoes in Europe.

Characteristics include periodic but unexpected eruptions, outbursts of something that has been simmering for a while and suddenly becomes unbearable; straightforwardness and a direct approach to addressing things that are askew, politically and strategically; communicative outbursts with impact; impactful letters or articles; explosive physical strength; visionary; endurance; action-oriented energy; eruptions within social media.

Forensically, it refers to the volcano Etna and Etna, Sicily, as a geographical location; an eruption or outburst within the political or social media arena; barking or howling dogs or wolves; losses within a legal context.

The orbital period a is 7 years and 325 days.

ENCELADE PRÉCIPITÉ SOUS LE MONT ETHNA.

Enceladus burried under Mount Æthna.

Enceladus unter dem Berg Æthna bedeckt.

Enceladus onder den Berg Ethna bedekt.

2483 GUINEVERE

Misfortune, pain, sorrow on the level of love and, consequently, a significant portion of life fulfillment; brilliant metaphysical insights that lead to conflicts or accidents; frustrations regarding ones love and sex life resulting in embitterment or behavioral deformations

Guinevere is a dark and elongated Hilda asteroid with a diameter of approximately 44 kilometers. Its discovery dates back to August 17, 1928, when the German astronomer Max Wolf identified it at the Heidelberg Observatory, initially assigning it the provisional designation 1928 QB. This asteroid was named after Guinevere, the wife of King Arthur and the lover of Lancelot in Arthurian legend. This affair led to civil war between King Arthur and his chief knight, who rescued Guinevere from burning at the stake and initiated the downfall of Arthur's idyllic kingdom. The name was suggested by Frederick Pilcher, and the proposal was submitted by Edward Bowell, who also made the object's key identification. The approved naming citation was published by the Minor Planet Center on 24 July 1983 (M.P.C. 8064). Notably, through numerical integration, it has been determined that Guinevere holds the distinction of being the Hilda asteroid with the highest likelihood of colliding with another asteroid. A significant portion, approximately 74%, of this impact risk occurs when Guinevere is in close proximity to perihelion, making its approach towards the main-belt asteroids.

It is astonishing how the symbolism of tragic love and the conflict associated with the legendary Guinevere is reflected in the discovery chart. Eros *(passion)* is precisely squared by Saturn conjunct Black Moon. Venus *(connection, love, sex)* is conjunct Sophrosine in Virgo *(which is neat, socially and ethically correct)* and square Apophis *(undergo intense terror)* square Hidalgo *(losing all stability)*. The discovery-Sun and Moon are both in Earth signs, Taurus and Virgo respectively, which hinders flexibility with heaviness. The Sun is conjunct Dziewanna *(deep painful experiences, profound suffering)* / Admetos *(untamed, excessive emphasis on the integrity of one's own passion or that of the sex partner)* / Cupido *(making amorous contact, daring to set aside reason and embrase a little madness)* / Dionysus *(intoxication, enlightenment through letting go)* / Chrisodom (here: *intelligent, witty)* / Paranal *(the struggle between the small human will and the greater powers in the world)*. The North Node is conjunct Mars *(coming into contact with individuals linked to action, courage, struggle, war, conflict, fire, iron)*. The position of Guinevere in the discovery chart was in the third degree of Pisces conjunct Sethos *(feeling cursed, misfortune coming from external sources)*. In short, this is not a good predisposition for a happy marriage or love life but rather the opposite:

bad luck, pain, sorrow in love, and thus a significant portion of bitterness and frustration related to love, bonding, sex and the base of ones existence. The only faint glimmer in this dark distribution of aspects is that Uranus in Aries is trine Lempo in Sagittarius *(ingenious metaphysical insights)* – which, however, can easily lead to conflicts due to the opposition of Uranus with Toro *(dangerous abruptly diverging energy, accidents).*

Forensically, Guinevere refers to the mythical queen of the same name or (high-ranking) individuals who find themselves in a tragically skewed relationship between their socio-economic status and their chronically neglected private needs.

The orbital period is 7 years ans 333 days.

3990 HEIMDAL

The Apocalypse; Zeitgeist-reality clash; epidemics, real or fictional; chaos magic; psychosomatic tension states and their eruption; channeling

Heimdal was discovered on September 25, 1987, by Poul Jensen and has a diameter of 35.68 km. Heimdall or Heimdallr, indirectly after whom the asteroid is named, is in Norse mythology the guardian of the gods, the son of nine virgin sisters, daughters of Aegir. Snorri Sturluson mentions Odin as his father. Heimdall arises from the foam of the surf, creating a connection (rain) bow from Midgard to Asgard called Bifröst, consisting of vapor and light. According to the myth, Heimdall has absolute hearing, hears the grass and wool grow, and blows a horn. As the guardian of the gods, Heimdall needs very little sleep, able to see a hundred miles both day and night. Heimdall is known as the white god because his skin is whiter than that of any other god, and his teeth are golden. At times, he takes on the form of a ram.

In its discovery chart, asteroid Heimdal is in the 10th degree of Pisces, conjunct the star Situla (the bucket or jug that Aquarius holds), conjunct Damocles/Aletheia/Cyllarus in a very tight opposition to Asbolus/Nessus/Thereus, all in 10 Virgo. The discovery Sun is in trine with Pholus. In this context, Heimdal represents a peculiar configuration of uncontrollable Centaur energies that, reinforced by Damocles, results in a highly nervous homeostasis, one that could discharge into something akin to 'Ragnorøk' at any given moment. The mix of Asbolus/Nessus/Thereus combines the heavy, dark energy of Asbolus with the violating or bloody nature of Nessus and the untamed sexual wildness and explosive brute force of Thereus, opposing 'Mr. Chaos': Damocles. Taking place on the Virgo-Pisces axis, interpreting this becomes challenging, except that Virgo, of all signs, would temper the wild energy of the Asbolus/Nessus/Thereus conjunction the most, and Pisces, being the sign of dissolution in the greater whole, puts Damocles in Pisces somewhat on the sidelines. In this context, Heimdal primarily relates to matters associated with the Virgo-Pisces axis: crystallization, routine work, service, health, illness, the physical, hygiene, detail, small pets, business, technology, etc. (Virgo), opposed to merging into other realms or dimensions, resolution, the final phase of things, beings, and processes, the spiritual or occult, behind-the-scenes occurrences, secret enemies or threats, large wild animals, music, art, eroticism, alcohol, and narcotics, etc. (Pisces).

When unleashing such tension on these two complementary psycho-spheres, the ticking time bomb goes off at the first significant affliction, and the ingredients of the Virgo-Pisces axis must be examined from the perspective of Pandora's box. Zeitgeist clashes (Pisces) and doomsday scenarios regarding illness are evident as potential outputs of Heimdal, always colored by the complete chart. On a smaller scale, Heimdal serves as a release valve within the psychosomatic, especially when dealing with prolonged psychosomatic conditions that finally experience a breakthrough or minor catastrophe. In a completely different context, Heimdal can be linked to chaos magic, and yet another, falling more within mundane astrology, relates to the outbreak of an epidemic among pets or large wild animals.

Francis Ford Coppola, film director of the movie *Apocalypse Now* has Heimdal in Capricorn in the first house conjunct Wood/Victoria/Hybris *(Vietnam/ Cambodia forests + helicopter attack with Wagner's Walküre music + blown-up Marlon Brando position)*; sextile Photographica/Hidalgo *(Dennis Hopper as ranting photojournalist off the rails)*; trine Quaoar *(Brando's bizarre unfolding construction of his own world)*; sextile Jupiter/Bienor *(gaining great fame with something)*; trine Toro *(concretization)*.

The Dutch 'state-virologist' Ab Osterhaus, known for annually acting as a national harbinger of doom by proclaiming a 'flu epidemic' in collaboration with the NOS Dutch state-news around the same period every year, marked a celebratory moment upon learning that a girl with a flu variant, potentially linked to vaccine sales, had been identified within the country. He expressed his joy by uncorking a whiskey bottle. Osterhaus has Heimdal on the Aries point, aligned with Cruithne/Crantor *(symbolizing 'End the Apocalypse' in the homeland)*, in square aspect to Pest in Capricorn *(emphasizing the need to take this officially recognized disease seriously)*, in opposition to Sisyphus *(highlighting the recurring nature of his announcements)*, square to Asbolus in Cancer *(eliciting an emotional response of horror)*, while also forming a sextile with Izhdubar *(representing useful failures)*, a sextile with Mjolnir, and a trine with Nemesis *(bad news)*.

Peter J. Carroll, the founder of postmodern chaos magic and the creator of the Illuminati of Thanateros, has Heimdal in Scorpio, conjoined with Psyche/Victoria/Eurydice/Pandora/2003 WL7; in opposition to Nessus/Klet and inconjunct Okyrhoe *(acceleration)/Kama sex)*. Typically, masturbation is employed to synchronize a chaos magical command with the orgasm, thereby implanting the command into the subconscious (Carroll also has Heimdal finally conjoined with Somnium, linked to the subconscious). Chaos magic involves extremely accelerated magical practices (Okyrhoe). Notably, within the apocalyptic context, the conjunction of Mars/Huya/BAM square Uranus *(explosive triggering of deep-seated karma)* in the discovery chart of Heimdal is intriguing.

The orbital period is 7 years and 301 days.

---

153 HILDA

Energy loss or energy manipulations, shyness, feeling separated from others; painful transformation processes, extremely empathetic

Hilda was discovered on November 2, 1875, by Johann Palisa. It is a large dark asteroid with a diameter of 170 km, composed of carbon compounds. The interpretation indicates: shyness, feeling separated from others due to excessive self-awareness in all situations, sensitivity, energy awareness, dark energy, concentric plutonic coercion, affinity with the dark side, or high sensitivity to dark developments, even in groups, often before others become aware, emphasizing.

Positive aspects: ability to protect oneself from external energy, ability to recharge oneself, talent for qi-gong, gong-fu, great strength, awareness of karmic aspects, and sharp mind. Negative aspects: energy loss due to others or environmental conditions, or neglect of oneself, psycho-energetic vampirism, difficulty socializing in a group, tendency towards narcotic substances, especially for socializing. Neutral: affinity with the dark, tendency to delve deeply, razor-sharp criticism.

Hilda always seems to demand a conscious and often painful transformation process, even with positive aspects. The asteroid has plutonic, Lilith-like characteristics, so it is radical and confrontational, resonating strongly with the heavy energies in the chart. Hilda-related issues have a negative impact on the heart, lungs, throat, nose, ear area, eyes, and teeth. A powerful daily practice of qi-gong is recommended for an afflicted or strong Hilda. Forensically linked to emos, depressing 80s music, energy vampires, or people who are victims of energy suckers.

The orbital period is 7 years and 336 days.

3514 HOOKE
The pain of Mother Earth is our pain

Hooke, with a diameter of 22 km, was discovered by Luboš Kohoutek on October 26, 1971. Hooke elevates consciousness in a highly idealistic, progressive, and humane manner. A dominant Hooke emerges as a freedom-loving creative spirit in an environment and era where the unrestrained power of the wild nature is broken and sterilized by powerful, oppressive system development, whether technical, chemical, bureaucratic, or military, behind the scenes or not. Hooke is a bit like a butterfly skillfully flying between the blades of a threshing machine as the earth darkens.

The asteroid primarily relates to our inner world, in turbulent reaction to an external world where the vibe of Earth and nature, and thus the essence of life itself, is seemingly beaten out. A significant part of us still resonates with this natural earthly reality, and most of the pain experienced by this part is initially caused unconsciously (via the madness of the zeitgeist). Hooke challenges us to transcend the need to preserve the peace at all costs because there is a necessity to defend ourselves against too much detachment from the natural reality from which we originate.

At the same time, Hooke warns with Eris conjunct Chiron in the discovery chart about unwavering resistance and standing firm, thus leading to estrangement from one's own nature. Hooke represents nature fighting back with human brains.

The asteroid was discovered in the 7th degree of Taurus, conjunct the truth and freedom-loving Hippy conjunction Orius/2003 CO1. The discovery Sun is in the third degree of Scorpio, conjunct Quaoar/Varda, opposite Thereus/Typhon/Sedna, and square Mors-Sumnus. The North Nodes are in Aquarius, while Libra and Scorpio are purged by both Black Moons. Hooke attracts a kind of dark apocalyptic scenario of the genre depicted in the film *HOME*, where Earth destruction by multinational corporations is shockingly portrayed.

The fight against this planet destruction must be waged and won, whether we like it or not. Hooke seems to represent the poignant pain of this on the Taurus-Scorpio axis, where, here, Taurus, not Scorpio, governs the transcendent consciousness. On a more personal level, Hooke enhances intelligence and analytical ability, social sensitivity, and social involvement. In a negative sense, Hooke can lead to habits within a hedonistic framework that may harm the body, especially through improper eating and problems in the neck/throat region. In forensic astrology, Hooke may refer to a hook, something that is hooked (fish), a diversion, turn, being stuck somewhere, or an addiction or obligation that is difficult to break free from: hooked on something.

The orbital period is 7 years and 300 days.

190 ISMENE

Bringing about one's own problems or causing great misfortune due to personal fear or lack of accountability, sheeple behavior; inconsistency; dissonance between profile and behavior

Ismene was discovered on September 22, 1878, by Christian Heinrich Friedrich Petersen and measures 159 km in diameter (other estimates give 79.5 and 90 km). Ismene is named after the daughter of Jocasta and Oedipus from Greek mythology. Ismene plays a role in Sophocles' tragedy, Antigone. The prologue of this tragedy is a dialogue between Antigone and Ismene. Antigone wants to bury the body of Polyneices, her brother, even though this is forbidden by Creon. Ismene refuses by saying that, as women, they must simply submit to male rulers. Antigone is less obedient and does as she pleases, which she will pay for with her life. The name Ismene is derived from the Greek ισμη (isme) knowledge, although isme is used everywhere as a suffix for specifically defined concepts, systems, lifestyles, organized activities, ideologies, artistic movements, and other phenomena, including disease symptoms.

Characteristics: Enjoying people in a social environment; attaching great importance to personal appearance and presentation; giving practical advice to others that is not followed oneself; a preoccupation with the problems and situations of others; having a pronounced opinion and plans but not implementing them due to a lack of courage; prudishness; sheeple behavior; making others victims of one's own cowardice; causing someone's death due to one's own fear, cowardice, or tendency to adhere to consensus; schizoid shifting between one's own profile and actual behavior; ruining one's own chances due to inertia or the inability to overcome one's own fear of life; conservatism that leads to suffering, disasters, and accidents; avoiding responsibility.

With a dominant Ismene, one must free oneself from dogmas, etiquette, decorum over substance, in short, all negative Saturn qualities. Fear is the opposite of accountability. Forensically, Ismene may indicate forced evacuations in disasters, explicitly disasters linked to human negligence arising from conservatism or bureaucracy; women who submit slavishly to men. Procrastination in taking responsibility for oneself is often the downfall of Ismene.

The orbital period is 7 years and 345 days.

9829 MURILLO
Lion-like courage, direct; drugs; sex; strong aversion to false communication; quick-witted

Murillo belongs to the subcategory of the Schubart-asteroids. It was discovered on September 19, 1973, by Cornelis Johannes van Houten, Ingrid van Houten-Groeneveld, and named after Bartolomé Esteban Murillo (1618-1682), who created a large number of religious paintings for churches. The painter from Seville is most famous for his genre paintings of children who are poor but happy, which continue to be imitated to this day.

Murillo is a very complex asteroid that is challenging to summarize into a core quality. On one hand, it is linked to needy and poor children and to the Sun, particularly dispelling the negative through the 'sunny and Lion-like' qualities. It calls for addressing and taking action against incorrect or inhumane situations. The conjunction in the discovery chart with the 'man-or-mouse Centaur' Rhiphonos in the 12th degree of Aries strengthens the positive Lion impulsiveness/action. Additionally, forensically, Murillo is linked to the

BARTHOLOMEUS MORILLUS HISPALENSIS
SE-IPSUM DEPINGENS PRO FILIORUM VOTIS AC PRECIBUS EXPLENDIS.
NICOLAUS OMAZURINUS ANTVERPIENSIS
Tanti VIRI simulacrum in Amicitiæ Symbolon
in æs incidi Mandauit. Anno 1682.

transmutation of metals and, in some charts, references to the painter Murillo or his religious and social themes.

With Pindarus, discovered on the same day as Murillo, the asteroid shares completely different qualities. Murillo falls under the sexual asteroids, with sexuality expressed more fifth-house-like; deriving pleasure from sex, recreational sex. There is a connection with drugs, drug trafficking, or getting involved in the drug world, but this impulse can also be about helping children with drug problems. Furthermore, there is a strong spiritual tendency, with spiritual experiences that are difficult to articulate or strongly clash with the norms or understanding of the social and cultural structure in which one is embedded. There is also a significant gap between the ideal and reality or concretization.

Nevertheless, Murillo enhances self-expression and generally links creativity to humanitarianism. Like Pindarus, Murillo has an aversion to unfair communication and impurities in that area, although people with both a strong Murillo and Pindarus may be drawn to the advertising profession, information, or public relations. For Murillo, advertising is particularly interesting due to the creative aspect. Murillo strongly reacts to people who don't walk their talk, beat around the bush, lie, or come with false pretenses, and politicians and opinion leaders from the mainstream media are at least critically heard. In a negative or irritated mood, Murillo can be very blunt and direct, or at least very straightforward. Murillo has a lot of willpower once the course is set, a tense Mercurial influence, and the asteroid accelerates cognitive and verbal abilities. With affliction, the nervous system suffers, especially the intestines and the head with hair loss due to stress or issues with teeth or ears.

The orbital period is 7 years and 330 days.

1144 ODA

Wealth accumulation; chemical giants, food industry, food adulteration with chemistry or genetic engineering; extreme behavior, sexual deviations, the need to balance mind and body

Oda was discovered on January 28, 1930, by Karl Wilhelm Reinmuth of the University of Heidelberg. The asteroid measures 57.59 km in diameter. The origin of the name Oda is unknown, but Oda was possibly a girl's name on a birthday calendar that he owned. Oda is a German form of the Old Germanic *audo* or *odo*, derived from *aud*, which means wealth or fortune.

Dominant in the personal horoscope, Oda favors the acquisition of wealth and riches and also a financial network, with three important caveats: Firstly, the predominantly blunt, excited nature and hardness must be restrained, as it can even lead to mental disorders and sexual pathology. With a dominant Oda, it is crucial to always ensure that mental work is proportionately combined with physical activity. This is a must with Oda, especially with significant afflictions. Additionally, any tendency towards status thinking, class division, discrimination, including sexual discrimination, must be unlearned. Finally, the energy of Oda must be sublimated into calm controlled work power, not least by engaging in music, even if only passively as someone who simply enjoys it from time to time.

Expansion, also financial, is strongly entrenched in this asteroid but must be kept pure. Oda, prominent in the horoscope, further increases the chance of an older life partner or a frigid woman and is forensically linked to financial networks such as the banking world and industry linking nutrition to chemistry. Physically, with affliction, Oda increases the likelihood of psychosomatic complaints, entity problems, or other energy problems, complaints from incorrect nutrition, food poisoning, blood poisoning, becoming a victim or perpetrator in a violent outburst, problems with the glandular system, heart, chest, or lungs.

With Oda, expressing oneself correctly or openly is often a problem. Instead, people with confronting situations with Oda may resort to excuses or say the opposite of what they mean. Especially in matters of love, this is a significant problem because they crave it. So, purging a bit of emotional and verbal cowardice is necessary, and the persona-I relationship must be kosher to experience fulfillment in love—not to end up like a sort of Citizen Kane. The negative caricature of Oda is the bulging rich manager of a chemical company or multinational food industry, a sociopath with sometimes wild statements, including homophobic ones, who eventually gets exposed and, despite his exemplary marriage, has been visiting gay bars for years.

Due to Oda's discovery position conjunct Phecda in the first degree of Virgo, Oda must be considered in forensic and/or mundane astrology because it can be a potentially significant player, especially in these times when companies like Monsanto, Bayer, and others threaten our environment and health, and the financial world has reached maximum collusion and criminality through a total fusion with politics worldwide. Elsbeth Ebertin wrote in 1928 about Phecda (Phacd, Phachd): "In combination with planetary malefics, it is said that this star can be a possible cause of 'a great bloodbath'. In combination with Neptune and with relevant configurations with the Moon, Venus, and Mars, it indicates a pathological sexual nature". Elsbeth Ebertin also noted that when the murder of the Austrian crown prince Franz Ferdinand took place in Sarajevo, Mars had just passed a conjunction with Phecda. A similar conjunction Mars-Phecda occurred during the flooding of the Vienna Palace of Justice between July 20 and 24, 1924, while riots were taking place everywhere else. [Source: *Fixed Stars and Their Interpretation*, Elsbeth Ebertin, 1928, p.53, under Phacd.]

The orbital period is 7 years and 95 days.

39382 OPPORTUNITY
Calculated power expansion, state tactics; seizing an opportunity

Opportunity was discovered on September 24, 1960, by Cornelis van Houten, Ingrid van Houten-Groeneveld, and Tom Gehrels, and the diameter is estimated to be 3 to 7 km. Astrologers have linked Opportunity to the concept of 'opportunity or chance', which is accurate in forensic astrology. However, in personal astrology, the positive luster of the term opportunity or chance is lost when associated with 'cool calculation, ruthless tactics', or 'strategic repression by the ruling system, prevailing norm, or state/government'.

Opportunity also has a harsh, coarse, intrusive energy that can manifest itself in rape (literally and figuratively). Furthermore, Opportunity can be associated with white-collar crime and politically covered military crimes. In the discovery chart, the Sun is conjunct the psychopathic Balbastre, and Nessus is trine Taurinensis.

The orbital period is 7 years and 326 days.

5928 PINDARUS

Criticizing immorality or false values; drug trafficking; sex scandals; strong aversion to false communication or manipulative and deceptive verbal communication; quick (trade) mind; accidents

Pindarus, like Murillo, was discovered on September 19, 1973, by Cornelis Johannes van Houten, Ingrid van Houten-Groeneveld, and Tom Gehrels, and named after the Greek poet Pindar of Thebes (c. 522 – c. 443 BC). Pindarus has many similarities in interpretation with Murillo, but its discovery position on the star Algenib makes Pindarus more negative in its effects, susceptible to scandals, violence, setbacks, poverty, or accidents, especially immorality.

Pindarus also falls under the lighter class of sexual asteroids, with sexuality at Pindarus being less associated with pleasure than with Murillo, and rather Pindarus incites various passions. The asteroid only does this when the energy is positively directed. Pindarus, however, increases the likelihood of involvement in a sex scandal. In a positive sense, it can manifest as erotic poems. There is also a connection with drugs, drug trafficking, or getting involved in the drug world, especially concerning cocaine. Here, too, this impulse can be about helping children with drug problems, but unlike Murillo, the risk of linking drugs to decay, the underworld, violence, or crime is significantly higher with Pindarus. Then, just like Murillo, there is a spiritual tendency, with spiritual experiences that are difficult to articulate or strongly clash with the norms or the level of understanding of the social structure or culture in which one is embedded. However, with Pindarus, this sometimes turns into sharp criticisms of mainstream spirituality and state religions (or creative heresy). Between the ideal and reality or concretization, there is also a large gap with Pindarus.

There is an extreme aversion to the stealth tactics of the media to influence people against their will, and a sharp, alert perception of wrongdoings in this regard. In a positive sense, this is the greatest strength of Pindarus. Pindarus sees through TV, newspapers, media training influences, official truths, advertising, PR, and other forms of communication that are essentially engaged in a soft but compelling form of brainwashing or communicative 'rape'. In some forensic charts, Pindarus may point to Pindaros or his work or poems or poetry, but this will be rare. In periods of stress, Pindarus can make one reckless regarding money and energy, and this asteroid, when frustrated, can become much more dramatic than Murillo. Therefore, a strong Pindarus requires the necessary self-control training.

The orbital period is 7 years and 346 days.

89903 POST
Post; postal affairs; "do no evil"; interpreting spiritual information into communicative

Post was discovered on February 20, 2002, by Berton L. Stevens. It measures 7.9 km in diameter. Post increases awareness of good and evil and insight into solving black-and-white contrasts. This asteroid enhances spiritual intelligence, making one witty, sharp, strategic, visionary, and capable of communicating spiritual matters with humor. Post also imparts a kind of social worker-like inclination to help men struggling with their homosexual identity.

A strong Post in an occult-oriented chart provides an excellent and constructive predisposition for the development of remote viewing, and in a more philosophical chart for futurological ecology, i.e., calibrating economy and lifestyle to the ecological factor. Post also stimulates nostalgia for groups or associations one was once a part of but that disbanded, such as a friends' club from college days, and may involve providing for a large group's needs. There is a certain threshold for human-spiritual values with Post, and when the occasion arises, someone with a strong Post can abruptly pull the plug on a process where these values have been violated for some time. On the contrary, someone with a dominant but heavily afflicted Post may hold bizarre pride, group hatred, or racist ideas.

Due to the discovery conjunct Regulus and Phecda, this predominantly positive asteroid hides a certain catch. This will mostly come to light during conjunctions with bodies that provide a harsh, cold, and ambitious drive or Centaurs that provoke the negative, especially black-and-white thinking, like an irritated Cyllarus, Teharonhiawako, or Cruithne. In forensic horoscopes and personal horoscopes, Post generally refers to "what comes after (...)" or the whole spectrum of mail, postal affairs, working in postal services, mail delivery and carriers, posting things (on social media), received mail, staying on top of things, etc. In English, 'post' also refers to a pole or mailbox.

The orbital period is 7 years and 331 days.

1911 SCHUBART

Intensity, short temper, aggressive, impulsive actions; extremely allergic to authorities or one's own authority aggressively undermined; revolutionary; 'fuck the system'; very harsh and difficult to handle energy; extreme vindictiveness and retaliation

Schubart belongs to the Hilda-subcategory of the Schubart-asteroids, who own their name to this object. It was discovered by Paul Wild on October 25, 1975, with a diameter of 80.09 km, and it is named after the German astronomer Joachim Schubart.

Characteristics include intensity, a short temper, aggression, impulsive actions; an extreme allergy to authorities or aggressive undermining of one's own authority; revolutionary; 'fuck the system'; very harsh and difficult-to-handle energy; extreme vindictiveness and retaliation. This is an extremely martial asteroid, mainly suitable for boxers or martial arts specialists who, in dominant positioning, will generally knock out the opponent at the first contact.

At the time of discovery, Schubart was conjunct the star Menkar *(danger, violence, uncontrolled impulses, etc.)* and Tisiphone *(revenge, retaliation)* in the 15th degree of Taurus. The discovery Sun was conjunct Bowell/Savage *(powerful and wild)* in the 2nd degree of Scorpio, in a close opposition to Mars/Tyson/Amor *(wanting to deliver a blow for personal reasons)* in the 2nd degree of Taurus.

Michael Peterson, the British criminal with the longest incarceration record in the UK, had Schubart in almost exact conjunction with Cyllarus *(identity crisis*: Peterson consistently called himself Charles Bronson) in the 8th degree of Scorpio, directly opposite Phaeton *(losing control, not being able to manage something)*/Taurinensis *(strategic insight)* in the 8th degree of Taurus. Peterson spent a total of 22 years in 120 prisons because he repeatedly got himself into trouble by beating up guards, leading to an extension of his sentence each time.

The orbital period is 7 years and 351 days.

8130 SEEBERG

Deep spiritual consciousness and growth; recreating and unfolding a new spiritual structure of a higher level than the old; detecting mental-psycho-energetic impurities; sensitive to psychic pressure differences; the succubus-incubus theme, gas explosions

Seeberg was discovered on February 27, 1976, by Freimut Börngen. A highly spiritual asteroid in the true sense of the word (liberation from obsessors and love for life, humanity, and creation). If strongly aspected, Seeberg provides an almost superhuman depth and insight.

Characteristics include understanding, analyzing, and purging the spiritual environment, recreating and unfolding a new spiritual structure of a higher level than the old; sensitivity to psychic pressure differences or shifts and detecting mental-psycho-energetic impurities in one's own homeostasis or that of others or the environment/spirit of the times; love over hate; consciousness transcending the rat race and postmodernisms and reanchoring in the human; the mysteries of Venus and connecting force; offering angelic comfort; being original, creative, possessing psychic intelligence and strength; magnetization, working with subtle energy; abrupt spiritual or esoteric breakthroughs; visionary or clairvoyant, remote viewing.

In forensic astrology, Seeberg may indicate a gas explosion, especially linked to traffic, transport, export, or air travel/space exploration. Gas explosions in the cosmos also fall under this. Seeberg is also the only asteroid, to my knowledge, linked to the succubus phenomenon via the position of Ginevra (female spirits) in the sex degree 17 Pisces conjunct Hidalgo; inconjunct Randi; semi-sextile Walpurga and trine North Moon's Node in Scorpio conjunct Hekate.

The orbital period is 7 years and 362 days.

37452 SPIRIT

Enthusiasm, motivational, that's the spirit!; bridge between two worlds; mitigating influence on violence

Spirit was discovered on September 24, 1960, by Cornelis Johannes van Houten, Ingrid van Houten-Groeneveld, based on material from Tom Gehrels. Spirit was named after the American space probe Spirit, with an estimated diameter of up to 9 km. Characteristics include enthusiasm, motivational, that's the spirit!; a bridge between this and the astral world (discovery Sun opposite Altjira; Pluto conjunct Interamnia); spiritual and mental energy; a mitigating influence on violence.

Spirit itself was discovered in the 11th degree of Aries, conjunct Osiris/Eris/Schadow under the influence of the star Erakis. Forensically, it may indicate enthusiastic individuals, a spirit (apparition), or an inspiration.

The orbital period is 7 years and 307 days.

499 VENUSIA

Softening; restoring the balance between inner needs and social, economic, or societal obligations; burnout prevention

Venusia (minor planet designation: 499 Venusia) is an asteroid in the outer asteroid belt, discovered by Max Wolf on December 24, 1902, in Heidelberg. Its diameter is 81 km (50.6 miles), and it is a dark P-type asteroid with an average distance from the Sun of 4 AU (600 million km). The asteroid is named in reference, not to Venus, but to the island of Venusia, or Hven, now Ven, located in the Øresund Strait between Denmark and Sweden. This island was given by King Frederick II to Tycho Brahe in 1576 for his observatories Uraniborg and Stjerneborg. Miss Bruhns, the daughter of Karl Christian Bruhns, named the asteroid during a visit in 1904 to Lund by participants of a meeting of the Astronomische Gesellschaft. The island is also honored by the asteroids (379) Huenna and (1678) Hveen.

Characteristics include softening, softening specifically related to timely breaking or interrupting Saturnine striving patterns; rat race behavior that breaks the connection with one's inner self and needs, causing a loss of self-control; burnout prevention. Venusia aims to restore balance between career and private life, ensuring healthy energy distribution. It is not undermining ambition; on the contrary, it ensures a healthy balance with private life and the reality of the intimate, personal self. Venusia also promotes diplomacy, tact, and has an affinity for poetry. It is a proactive energy, favorable for climbing the social ladder through influential contacts due to its conjunction with Sirius in the discovery chart. Forensically Venusia may denote things or events that are withing the psychosphere of Venus, or simply the island Venusia.

The orbital period is 8 years and 11 days.

1941 WILD
Directionlessness combined with a lack of impact; wild

Wild belongs to the subcategory of the Schubart-asteroids and was discovered by Karl Reinmuth on October 6, 1931, with a diameter of 17.12 km. The asteroid, named after Swiss astronomer Paul Wild, mainly refers to wild in forensic astrology. In the natal chart, Wild seems to combine a sense of directionlessness with a desire to make an impact, yet failing to do so.

The discovery Wild is in the 14th degree of Aries inconjunct Mars/BAM in the 14th degree of Scorpio, with Mars/BAM forming a square with Pandora. The feeling of missing opportunities can turn into action and tackling issues when indecisiveness (strong Libra influence in the discovery chart) is overcome (or forced). Forensically, Wild may also indicate wild animals or hunting game.

The orbital period is 7 years and 340 days.

Mentr'el tuo Padre in quella, en questa parte   Tuoi d'abbondantia empiſti, e' tal fu l'arte
Seguiſti o' Roma, e' mentre i membri umti   Che' ne trabocco'l teuere ei sue liti
Teneſti del tuo corpo, ognun di Marte   Gran segni ancor ne'l uentre tuo ſi uede
T'aueua per figlia e' trionfando i siti   Che' oia teneſti 'l mondo. sotto 'l piede

CYBELE ASTEROIDS

---

229 ADELINDA
Highly context and connotation-sensitive in partnerships, relationships, and contacts; alternately sensitive and flamboyantly inspired; solution-oriented; refined; appreciates the finer things in life; allergic to monotony; ambitiously works to transcend the chaos experienced in current existence

A large dark C-type asteroid with a diameter of 93 km, discovered on August 22, 1882, by Johann Palisa. Adelinda exerts a predominantly gentle feminine influence and has an association with shields, protection, defense, and lindens, lindenwood, and linden blossoms. At the time of discovery, Adelinda was in the 2nd degree of Pisces influenced by the star Ancha and conjunct Sila-Nunam. Adelinda further enhances refined, sensitive context, and connotation sensitivity; values the better things in life; provides enjoyment in studying, where there is great enthusiasm and commitment, provided it involves a study that constantly challenges, with plenty of growth and discovery opportunities. Monotony and excessive superficiality are considered deadly and cause restlessness. Work that requires equal commitment from both emotion and intellect and offers variety is essential.

Adelinda prefers quiet environments and outdoor activities, especially hiking through pristine nature. Calming the thoughts and staying focused is a challenge with a strong Adelinda influence. There is a strong aversion to pulp TV. When afflicted, issues with the lungs or respiratory system may arise, or difficulty in shielding or indicating personal boundaries. Adelinda may also develop a tendency towards sweetness and indulgence, especially under stress. Some natural remedies that are safe for others, may not work or have adverse effects in individuals strongly influenced by Adelinda, unless they are self-invented or discovered. When afflicted with the Sun in the natal chart, there is a chance of hip problems and allergic reactions when drinking linden blossom tea; tightness in the chest, breathing problems.

The orbital period is 6 years and 118 days.

420 BERTHOLDA

Being highly dependent on positive or negative aspects, resulting in either difficulties or success in the social sphere and self-expression; finding it either easy or difficult to maintain one's own course; an inability to fully control a technical system or exert complete control over it; obsession with sex and unusual sexual activities containing a substantial range of ways and activities for sexual self-expression; the option of great powerful rulership if the libido is controlled in a healthy way. A fusion of both is also possible, leading to significant corruption of the Caligula genre

Bertholda is a large main-belt asteroid with a diameter of 141 km. Discovered by Max Wolf on September 7, 1896, in Heidelberg, Germany, the object is classified as a P-type asteroid. In the Tholen classification, P-type asteroids are relatively rare and characterized by low albedo (reflectivity) in the visible spectrum and moderate albedo in the near-infrared. These asteroids are often associated with primitive or 'primitive-like' compositions, indicating a significant amount of carbonaceous materials. Bertholda was named after Berthold I of Zähringen (* around 1000; † November 6, 1078, in Weilheim an der Teck). Known as 'the Bearded', he was Duke of Carinthia from 1061 to 1077 and Margrave of Verona.

A strong Bertholda in the horoscope can instill a desire for self-expression and social positions that allow for a lot of contact with people, free from constraints and monotony. Although this asteroid elicits a desire to be spontaneous and natural, technical and methodical aspects are also attractive. Bertholda is friendly in nature, but a person with a strong influence of this asteroid may not enjoy complete ease in dealing with others due to difficulty expressing themselves. Although orderly and thorough, a strong Bertholda can also make it difficult to maintain the system and order one would like. There is a conflict between desires and expression, preventing a person's abilities from coming into their own. This lack of fulfillment of deeper qualities leads to oppression and frustration. Bertholda may, therefore, encourage a love of comfort foods like sweets, calorie-rich foods, as well as meat and starch, and any indulgence may cause skin disorders or possible intestinal problems. This schizoid precondition usually finds its cause in repressed sexual needs and wishes, which easily become an obsessive underskin condition. This condition strongly contrasts with the Virgonian core of this asteroid, which is very stable, solid and controlling and aimed at the preservation of libidinous energies instead of addictively giving in to them.

The Sun and Moon are conjunct in Virgo in the discovery chart and well-aspected. The extreme sexual urge roots in both the Venus-position of

Bertholda in the second degree Libra, conjunct Salacia *(masturbation)*/
Kytheria *(sex xxxl)*/Messalina *(sexual hunger and promiscuity)*, and in the
conjunction of Bertholda with Yarilo *(fertility, sex)* in 14 Pisces square Pluto.
However, despite the 'sex-thing' and the unstable underskin condition,
Bertholda may bestow someone with this asteroid dominant (conjunct Sun
or MC) with great and powerful rulership talents, with original, ingenious
insights, on condition that the libido is controlled and communicative
skills are trained (Pluto in Gemini square Sun/Moon) to express themselves
tactfully.

Jeffrey Epstein had Bertholda in 14 Aquarius conjunct North Nodes (Mean
Node/True Node - *meeting Bertholda type people*), Pepper *(assertive energy,
agitating)*, 1998 WU31 *(hunger for power)*, 2005 RR43 *(radicalism, planning
an attack)* Sethos *(curse)* and 2001 UR163 *(great vision but bad preparation
plus some clairvoyant talent)*. Epstein had an abnormal sex drive, and it seems
in retrospect that he wanted more than just a strong position to be able to
blackmail the top of politics, members of royal houses, and Big Industry but
wanted to bring them down completely, which would have succeeded if the
FBI had not deliberately made all the files disappear. The power lust, by the
way, is rooted in Epstein's Sun/Machiavelli-conjunction in the first degree
Aquarius square Amycus *(Plutonian lust for power)* in the anaretic degree of
30 Aries, but it is beyond dispute that in his horoscope the asteroid Bertholda
had a decisive tactical role in his existence. Epstein had a painting on the
wall depicting himself in prison as a bizarre prophecy. For the visitors to his
island of lust, their heaven turned into hell (Sethos). A problem they solved by
murdering him in jail, making the press say he hanged himself, and 'deleting'
his records and videos.

Forensically, dark black and white photographs, old photographs, nude
photography in a dark, pornographic or menacing to romantic, dystopian
or occult style; porn stars, sex addicts M/F; femme fatales; opinion leaders
or influencers with very high popularity – often within a sexual connotation
(Social media icon Kim Kardashian has Bertholda in the anaretic degree 30
Cancer, conjunct Vertex; sextile MC/Jupiter; square Sun in Libra); great (or
corrupt) leaders or rulers.

The orbital period is 6 years and 114 days.

107 CAMILLA
Empathy, compassion; a sudden breakthrough of futurological engineering

Camilla was discovered on November 17, 1868, by Norman Robery Pogson and measures 285 x 205 x 170 km. Camilla has a moon with a diameter of 11 km, provisionally designated as S/2001 (107) 1. The asteroid is named after the mythical Camilla. The name is presumed to be Etruscan, and its meaning is unclear, with no known direct relation to the Latin Camillus (a youth in the service of religion). In Virgil's Aeneid, Camilla is the daughter of King Metabus and Casmilla. Expelled from his throne, Metabus, carrying his young daughter in his arms, is pursued into the wilderness by rebellious Volsci (the Italian tribe of which he is king). The river Amasenus blocks his path, and, fearing for the well-being of the child, Metabus ties Camilla to his spear and throws her across, invoking the help of Diana and promising that Camilla will serve her if she saves his daughter. Camilla is nursed by a mare, learns to handle a spear and bow from her first steps, and grows up in the company of her father and the shepherds in the hills and forests. Virgil wrote that Camilla, once grown, was so swift on her feet that she could traverse a field of grain without breaking the tops of the plants under her feet and run over water without getting wet.

In the radix chart, Camilla seems to indicate two divergent things: on the one hand, empathy, social compassion, sensitivity, and a helpful attitude. On the other hand, the asteroid points to realizing a dream through engineering, inventions related to anticipating a blind spot in technology, problem-solving through transcending the problem, futurological inventions or innovations, unleashing a significant acceleration, or stimulating expansion or international recognition. With affliction, there may be frustration over unnecessary bureaucratic delays of a good idea or solution that many people are clamoring for, or problems with fluid balance or water retention around the ankles.

The inventor of the hovercraft, Christopher Cockerell, had Camilla in the 26th degree of Virgo conjunct 2003 OP32 *(out-of-the-box prophet)*, including a trine to Uranus *(inventions, the new)*/Altjira *(dream world)*; square to Pluto *(opposing power)*; opposition to Eris/Ceto/2000 QB243 *(perseverance to the end in improving an invention related to water or distance)*. Cockerell went through a long period of testing and improvements until he had the final hovercraft, invested a lot of his own money in the project, and then had to lobby extensively to get his invention into production after the British government showed little interest for a long time.

Forensically: things or situations related to a safe or fast crossing (over water); things that fly over the water.

The orbital period is 6 years and 178 days.

3015 CANDY

Sweets, sweetness, sweeteners; a very firm certainty about the cause of something perceived as negative, wrong, or a nuisance; addiction to the negative

Candy was discovered on November 9, 1980, by Edward Bowell, and has a diameter of 24.5 km. Named after the astronomer Michael P. Candy, this asteroid, when considered forensically, relates to sweetness and candy. However, in the natal chart, Candy takes on a different meaning, signifying a very strong certainty regarding the cause of something perceived as negative, wrong, or a nuisance. This 'insight' can become an addictive standpoint. Many people are addicted to negativity, explaining why news in newspapers and on TV is still tolerated and consumed, as well as many TV series revolving around power games or violence. This negative aspect serves as a kind of life necessity for most people (with mainstream media acting as a utility) to channel their gut feelings. The adults' need for negativity, which they comment on with their 'insight' into its cause, is comparable to the sweet-keeping function of candy for children.

The discovery Sun of Candy is in the 18th degree of Scorpio, conjunct Pandora/Eureka/Unruh/Irus; square Mors-Somnus; sextile Wilson-Harrington. Candy itself was in the second degree of Taurus at the time of discovery, conjunct the star Mira (the miraculous).

The orbital period is 6 years and 84 days.

65 CYBELE

Sacrifice of the masculine to the feminine; aversion to cocky behavior; inclination towards metaphysics; incest; relationships with significant age differences; inability to accept one's own aging process

Cybele was discovered by Ernst Wilhelm Tempel on March 8, 1861, and measures 302×290×232 km. Cybele has one moon with a diameter of 11 km, orbiting the asteroid at a distance of 917 km. Originally an Anatolian Magna Mater figure, a Mother Earth goddess/Mountain goddess, related to many other Mother goddess figures, Cybele later gained a self-castrating priestly following.

Characteristics: liquidation or sacrifice of the masculine to the feminine; castration; subjugation of man; aversion to macho behavior and advocacy for the opposite; intense dislike of cocky behavior or male assertiveness and power display; false women's emancipation; commercial 'spirituality'; commercial gurus; the antithesis of patriarchal religions (state religions); a greater preoccupation with sexuality as life progresses and a more mature and adult perspective on the female-male polarity, striving for synergy.

In Cybele, there is a serious inclination towards metaphysics and the ability to comprehend complex metaphysical or magical principles (reality creation). The prominent aspect of Cybele that emerges depends on the overall horoscope. Other astrologers have associated Cybele with incest, significant age differences between sexual partners, such as grandmother-grandson relationships, fetishizing a person or attribute, damaging one's self-esteem, inability to accept one's own aging (and the corresponding behavior), and homosexuality.

The orbital period is 6 years and 138 days.

---

76 FREIA
Great beauty and attraction, a sexy appearance and stimulation, fertility

Freia is considered one of the sexual asteroids. The asteroid has a connection with great beauty and attraction, a sexy appearance and stimulation, fertility, and (whether or not attainable) young blonde women with black nylons or stockings. (Similar to how many Black Moon transits are associated with attractive dark-skinned women dressed in black and pink). There is also an association of Freia with witchcraft, the cat, and the wild boar.

Model and writer Susan Smit, who debuted in the Netherlands with the confession book *Heks* (Witch), has Freia conjunct Bennu/1998SM165/Ophelia; sextile Rhiphonos/1998WA25/Prometheus/Nike; square Datura/2001XA255 and trine Arachne/Bok. Freia is a very dark and large asteroid with a diameter of 183 km. It was discovered on October 21, 1862.

Freia has an orbital period of 6 years and 117 days.

522 HELGA

Deflowering; extreme sexual experiences; a relationship with a very brutal dominant partner, destructive relationships; privacy violations

Helga was discovered by Max Wolf on January 10, 1904, and measures 101.22 km. The asteroid was named by Th. Lassen, who calculated Helga's orbit at the time. Helga comes from Old Norse Helgi (holy or blessed). During the discovery, Helga was in the 29th degree of Cancer, conjunct the star Aludra (hymen); trine Sila-Nunam; square Bienor/1999 TD10/1995 QY9/1999 RA215; opposition to Bacchus/2005 UJ438. The discovery Nessus is on the sexual 17th degree of Pisces, conjunct Praamzius/Amor/Toro/Thisbe/Apollo/Aphrodite/Soomana, trine the parasitic 2002 PN34, and square the NLP-Plutino 1998 HK151 in Gemini, and relationship crisis asteroid Gorgo in Sagittarius. The Sun is in Capricorn, sextile Nessus, and opposition to 2002 PN34. Although there is an underlying fresh, clear nature and proactive energy in Helga, the interpretation mainly revolves around extremes in the relational-sexual sphere.

Characteristics: deflowering; extreme sexual experiences; a relationship with a very brutal dominant partner, destructive relationships; parasitic relationships, privacy violations. Depending on its placement in a passive or active house or sign, and in the context of the overall horoscope, a dominant Helga may be a victim or perpetrator or a combination of both in varying proportions. This is a highly extreme asteroid.

The orbital period is 6 years and 338 days.

225 HENRIETTA

Tactfully, friendly, social, outspoken, sense of humor, talent for performing as stand up comedian, Libra-like energy

With a diameter of 128 km, Henrietta stands as a prominent member of the outer main-belt asteroids, discovered by Johann Palisa in Vienna on April 19, 1882. It was named in honor of Henrietta, the wife of astronomer Pierre J. C. Janssen. Characterized as a C-type asteroid, it likely consists of primitive carbonaceous material, presenting an extreme dark surface with an albedo of 0.040.

Henrietta strongly placed in the chart (for example conjunct Sun, Moon or Ascendent) can stimulate a friendly and charming nature. However, its influence suggests a tendency to be easily swayed by others. While social and amiable, Henrietta can turn dogmatic and forceful under pressure, demonstrating a strong-willed and unwavering disposition. Independence is preferred, with a reluctance to shoulder heavy workloads or responsibilities.

In public roles, a strong Henrietta shines, leveraging a friendly demeanor, genuine interest in people, a sharp sense of humor and a desire to please. Someone with a dominant Henrietta may have a tendency to offering sound advice, but must be cautious about being overly opinionated in contentious matters. The astrological features of Henrietta align with potential physical weaknesses, particularly in fluids and head-related senses, leading to conditions like headaches, eye issues, dental problems, or severe sinus conditions. Additionally, vulnerabilities in the kidneys or bladder may be indicated. Forerensically Henrietta denotes women named Henrietta, or stand up comedians or public performers who integrate critisism on the government in their art.

The orbital period is 6 years and 88 days

121 HERMIONE

Transcending the emotional comfort zone by becoming mentally and verbally steadfast, stable, confident, and goal-oriented.

Hermione was discovered on May 12, 1872, by James Craig Watson. It is a large dark, carbonaceous asteroid measuring 268 x 186 x 183 km, with a small moon S/2002 (121) 1, ranging from 13 to 18 km in diameter, orbiting around it in 2 days, 13 hours, and 55 minutes. Hermione is derived from Hermes and roughly translates to messenger. She was betrothed to Neoptolemus, but when he was killed in the Trojan War by Orestes, she became his bride. The myth of Hermione revolves around themes of arranged marriage, losing the fiancé, and jealousy.

In the natal chart, Hermione seems to indicate the necessity of transcending the emotional comfort zone by becoming mentally and verbally steadfast, stable, confident, and goal-oriented. When Hermione is prominently aspected, life tends to throw various obstacles and crises on the path to effectuate this process, often involving a repetition of the essential same in ever-changing situations.

The orbital period is 6 years and 144 days.

260 HUBERTA

Sympathetic, social, superficial, directionless; finds it difficult to plan or handle money; has a sense of humor, self-mockery, and self-relativization; can stimulate artistry and creativity; periods of prosperity or progress start with a chaos phase in which boundaries are pushed. Can get very entangled in a social-emotional complex that grows bigger and bigger until it becomes a source of stress or suffocation

Huberta is a large asteroid, estimated 94 - 102 km in diameter. It is dark and rich in carbon and was discovered by Johann Palisa on 3 October 1886 in Vienna and was named after Saint Hubertus. Astrologically this asteroid is rather complex, despite the fact it does not belong to the heavyweights.Hubertus was a son of Bertrand, the Duke of Aquitaine, and led a worldly life. He went to the Neustrian court of Theuderic III in Paris but, like many nobles, moved to the Austrasian court in Metz due to Mayor Ebroin. There, he was warmly welcomed by Mayor Pepijn van Herstal and also received a high position. After the death of his wife Floribanne, during the birth of their son Floribertus, he withdrew to the Ardennes, where he indulged in hunting. On Good Friday of the year 683, he went hunting, even though it was a very disrespectful activity on that day. Hubertus noticed a large deer and chased it with his dogs. When he almost caught the deer and it turned towards him, he wanted to shoot it. At that moment, a shining cross appeared between the antlers. A voice told him to go to Lambertus of Maastricht. Saint Hubertus is now known as the patron saint of hunting. This legend only became associated with the life of Hubertus from the 15th century onwards. Because he once cured a man of rabies, he is especially invoked against this disease. For this purpose, the so-called Hubertus bread is also blessed. His feast day is celebrated on November 3.

A prominent presence of Huberta in the birth chart signifies a lively and spontaneous optimistic Libra/Sagittarius-like nature. It exudes a sense of humor, allowing for amusement in various situations, even at its own expense or that of others. Huberta bestows a musical and artistic inclination, making it a useful asteroid for individuals working in the entertainment field. With a generous and joyful disposition stimulated by Huberta, a strong influence of this asteroid makes it easy to form connections. However, when provoked, such an individual may exhibit a swift temper that quickly dissipates. Huberta also encourages a love for a good debate, and individuals with a strong influence of this asteroid may intentionally stir discussions for enjoyment.

However, there is also a strong emotional and scattered influence, which may lead a person to find themselves entangled in emotional situations against

rational judgment due to its compassionate and overly generous nature. In this way, Huberta may hinder material accumulation and personal happiness. Additionally, the asteroid instills a tendency to resist structure in general and financial planning, potentially leading to budgeting problems. These problems may also have their origin in being overly optimistic in combination with a certain chaotic entanglement in all kinds of wild ideas that are more original or challenging than realistically in line with one's true will (Mercury conjunct Jupiter/Pelion). With a strong Huberta, it is very important that one's energy output aligns strongly with one's dreams or ideals (Mars in exact opposition Neptune). Periods of prosperity or progress start with a chaos phase in which boundaries are pushed. Essentially, a crisis situation or trauma, in a paradox, releases just that inherent malnourished Saturn energy in Huberta that can provide direction and self-discipline.

In terms of health, Huberta can lead to a tendency to indulge in sugars and starches, which could affect the liver, kidneys, or skin, potentially resulting in issues like pimples or eczema. When afflicted, Huberta also makes prone to ptomaine poisoning, infections and energy losses or hemorrhoids or other problems in the anal zone. Psychologically there may be a strong tendency to emotional claiming. Forensically, Huberta points to women named Huberta, or men named Hubert; to Saint Hubertus; hunting, deer, antlers, and rabies; very popular memes based on female models or glamorous travel locations that circulate on social media. Finally, Huberta can denote very complex security or protection systems (Saturn in Cancer conjunct Quaoar).

The orbital period is 6 years and 142 days.

570 KYTHERA

Strong sexual drive, lust; a desire for quick money; accidents, violence, or injuries due to infatuation, doing the wrong things in a numb state

Kythera or Cythera was discovered by Max Wolff on July 30, 1905, and measures 102.81 km in diameter – although there are other estimates circulating that are smaller, around 87.49 km. The asteroid was named after Kythira, the Greek island at the bottom of the Peloponnese associated with Aphrodite in antiquity. The discovery chart also associates Kythera with Venusian events. Characteristics: very strong sexual drive, lust, desire for satisfaction, a tendency to want to earn quick money; a tendency towards drug use without necessarily falling into addiction; endurance and strength;

anal sex; desire for independence; addiction to masturbation. However, also indicates accidents, violence, or injuries due to infatuation, doing the wrong things in a numb state, or gas explosions. Forensically, Kythera is linked to pornography, porn actors, working in the sex industry, prostitution, the Amsterdam sex industry, and erotica based on nun costumes.

The orbital period is 6 years and 118 days.

319 LEONA
Passionate; seductive; great interest in occult and metaphysical subjects; sexual qi-gong; able to use significant lies to expedite processes

Leona was discovered by Auguste Charlois on October 8, 1891, and measures 68.16 km in diameter. Characteristics: exceptionally passionate, excitement; seductive, using seduction to rise or achieve goals; very interested in occult and metaphysical subjects; sexual qi-gong. Negatively: claiming through seduction, intrigues, femmes fatales; able to use significant lies to expedite processes. Sexual qi-gong specialist Mantak Chia has Leona conjunct Chiron *(healer, teacher)* in Virgo. His techniques primarily involve channeling and transforming sexual energy for increased vitality and a happier sex life.

The orbital period is 6 years and 89 days.

733 MOCIA
Daring to take a new step in unknown or new territory; keeping promises; the phase of transitioning from child to adulthood

Mocia was discovered by Max Wolff on September 12, 1912, and measures 98.49 km in diameter. The name Mocia is derived from Mok, the nickname of the discoverer's son. Mocia refers to the courage and desire to become independent, taking the initiative to stand on one's own feet, daring to take a new step in unknown or new territory; realizing that freedom is not the same as doing whatever comes to mind; being very conscientious about keeping one's word or promises; intense aversion to lies, piercing through lies; the phase of transitioning from child to adulthood; puberty. Forensically, Mocia mainly denotes the young man.

The orbital period is 6 years and 99 days.

---

401 OTTILIA

Light after darkness; the higher self manifesting; the refined, human state of consciousness 'Mensch', 'gentleman'; an angelic touch; the uncovering of blind spots and fatal errors; internal meaningful civilization (as opposed to cultural invasion and encapsulation); an indestructible natural belief in miracles and magic; healing of physical and mental health problems through psychosynthesis or spiritual-physical alignment

Ottilia was discovered by Max Wolf on March 16, 1895, in Heidelberg and has a diameter of 99 km. It is named after the Germanic folkloric character Saint Ottilia or Odile. Odile of Alsace, also known as Odilia or Ottilia, born around 662 - 720 at Mont Sainte-Odile, is a revered saint in the Catholic Church and the Eastern Orthodox Church. Hailing from the noble Etichonid family, Odile faced adversity from birth, being born blind. Cast aside by her father due to her gender and disability, she was raised by peasants in Palma. Miraculously, at the age of twelve, the itinerant bishop Erhard of Regensburg baptized her as Odile (Sol Dei), and she regained her sight. Despite familial challenges, including the accidental death and resurrection of her younger brother Hughes, Odile persisted. She sought refuge in a cave, escaping her father's wrath, and eventually returned to nurse him when he fell ill. Over time, she convinced him to establish the Mont Sainte-Odile Abbey, where she became abbess. Odile later founded Niedermünster, guided by a vision from St. John the Baptist. Despite hardships, including a fire in 1542, the local well at Niedermünster is believed to cure eye diseases. After describing the afterlife to her sisters, Odile took communion and peacefully passed away. She was buried at Ste. Odile, succeeded as abbess by her niece, Saint Eugénie d'Alsace.

Within the main frame of the Virgo-Pisces axis (Ottilia discovery position is 26 Virgo Retrograde opposite Sun in 27 Pisces), Ottilia imparts an eagerness for knowledge and an intense desire to contribute meaningfully to life. Keywords include clever, imaginative, analytical; a yearning for freedom from restrictions and outlets for restless qualities combined with an allergy for drudgery and monotony. Ottilia stimulates a reluctance to take advice and working alone or independently. At times, this asteroid influence may cause inner turmoil and mood swings, particularly when feeling misunderstood. As Ottilia deepens one's sensitivity, people who undergo a dominant influence of this asteroid may get easily hurt and offended. Overall, Ottilia may bestow a quiet intensity, challenging for others to comprehend, prompting one to be on guard against ridicule or criticism (Mercury trine Arawn). Also stimulated is a profound appreciation for the outdoors, relishing activities in nature's beauty. When afflicted, Ottilia may contribute to weaknesses in the heart, lungs, and bronchial area, potentially causing heart issues, pneumonia, asthma, or tuberculosis. Additionally, afflictions may create tension in the nervous system, particularly affecting the solar plexus and stomach, leading to nervous indigestion and related conditions.

Ottilia-themes are: light after darkness, the higher self manifesting, the refined, human state of consciousness 'Mensch', 'gentleman'; an angelic touch forms a leitmotiv within the influence of this asteroid. Other characteristics include: the uncovering of blind spots and fatal errors; internal meaningful civilization (as opposed to cultural invasion and encapsulation); an indestructible natural belief in miracles and magic (Uranus in Scorpio trine Eris in Pisces) and a cognitive acceptance of paranormal phenomena and occult 'world soul-tectonics' (Saturn in Scorpio trine Flammario/Orcus/Praamzius in Pisces); healing of physical and mental health problems through psychosynthesis or spiritual-physical alignment. The latter quality will be beyond imagination for some but is crucial, for example, in African and Afro-African magio-religions and any animistic religion in which ancestor worship is very important and connected to the here and now. Within that sphere, illnesses and periods of misfortune are often directly correlated to skewed relationships with ancestors, with the healing process consisting of reconciliation. Forensically, Ottilia can refer to St. Ottilia, eye doctors, blind people, opticiens; humanitarian processes or movements, or miracles.

The orbital period is 6 years and 44 days.

790 PRETORIA
Pretoria, South Africa; problems due to drugs or the drug world

Pretoria was discovered on January 16, 1912, by Harry Edwin Wood and measures 170.37 km in diameter. Primarily, this is a geographical asteroid (see the list in the back) referring to the South African city of Pretoria. In the natal chart, a dominant Pretoria indicates possible serious problems due to drug use or involvement in the drug world, including being liquidated or imprisoned for drug-related issues.

The orbital period is 6 years and 109 days.

643 SHEHERAZADE

Strong ambitious drive; non-compromising; independent; wants to build up something substantial; has many setbacks, but perseveres; has difficulty in realizing a full emotional connection with intimates or children; can start a conflict or in a mundane chart a war; can excel in deep psychological or spiritual surveys or professions

Scheherazade is a Cybele asteroid with a diameter of 71 km, discovered on September 8, 1907, by the German astronomer August Kopff in Heidelberg. The asteroid is named after the legendary Arabian storyteller Scheherazade from One Thousand and One Nights. Scheherazade has a name rooted in Middle Persian, specifically Čehrāzād, denoting 'lineage' and 'noble, exalted.' The evolution of her name is traced through various Arabic sources, with early renditions such as Shirazad and Shahrazad.

When the asteroid Sheherazade dominates a natal chart, it instills a strong desire for success and financial prosperity. Individuals influenced by Sheherazade exhibit drive and confidence, pursuing ambitions with unwavering determination and overcoming obstacles along the way. This asteroid directs thought processes towards entrepreneurship, business, and wealth accumulation, emphasizing practical matters over artistic or philosophical pursuits.

Key Sheherazade-themes encompass independence and a reluctance to take orders or seek advice, fostering a communication style marked by directness, frankness, and gruffness—traits that, incidentally, may lead to the loss of friendships due to the asteroid's forthright approach. Furthermore, Sheherazade can make it challenging to reciprocate kindness, compassion, or affection in close relationships, potentially causing tensions with those in one's immediate circle. Additionally, forming a close emotional bond with children may prove difficult for individuals dominated by this asteroid in their horoscope. Healthwise, vulnerabilities affect the senses of the head, contributing to issues like eye, ear, or sinus troubles, as well as concerns related to female organs.

Once the 'childhood diseases' have been overcome and someone has gained more trust in this energy, a deeper layer of the asteroid reveals itself. With Saturn conjunct Eris/Nessus in Pisces (combined with the discovery Sun - sextile Neptune - and Moon in Virgo) in the discovery chart, Sheherazade can positively excel in psychological deep-sea exploration requiring great perseverance or the unraveling of spiritual truths and illusions. Sheherazade combines a penchant for psychological or mystical knowledge with an offensive Saturnian hard-driven ambition for financial and material independence (Sheherazade occupied the 8th degree Aries and was conjunct Orcus during its discovery). These traits can conflict and complement each other, taking years to bring into synergy. Additionally, there is creativity present that can even lead to fame (through personal effort) with Bienor on the midpoint of Venus-Mars from two exact sextiles.

In worldly horoscopes, this asteroid can indicate a danger point due to its inherent aspect related to world wars: Saturn conjunct Eris in an exact square to Pluto, with Saturn making an opposition to Neoptolemus. Than Uranus is sextile Typhon. Uranus - Typhon connections are notoriously related to disasters like nuclear meltdowns and tsunamis.

Forensically: Sheherazade as a character; the storyteller; a behind-the-scenes trade war on the global stage; hard-nosed businesspeople; pioneering psychiatrists or psychologists.

The orbital period is 6 years and 57 days.

168 SIBYLLA

Fortune-telling in trance, seeing the blind spot or wound of the mind, or insight into the state of a deceased person who finds no peace

Sibylla was discovered on September 28, 1876, by James Craig Watson, conjunct the star Algenib, and measures 148.39 km in diameter. Sibylla is named after Sibyl (Greek Σιβύλλα, Latin Sibylla), in antiquity the term for women who, inspired by a deity (usually Apollo) and thus in ecstasy, spontaneously and unsolicitedly predicted the future.

Traits: fortune-telling or predicting in trance, spiritual ecstasy, prophetic statements during ecstasy; insight into the blind spot or wound of the mind or an understanding why a deceased person finds no peace in the post-mortum state. In negative aspects: scandals, violence, setbacks and poverty or false prophecies. Works best in favorable aspect with Neptune. Aspected with the Sun, the asteroid often indicates psychological problems or instability. Forensically Sibylla denotes a fortune-teller or medium.

The orbital period is 6 years and 75 days.

SIBYLLA LIBYCA

Æquus erit cunctis, gremio Rex membra reclinet Reginæ mundi Sanctus per secula uiuus.

566 STEREOSKOPIA

Perceiving things, processes, or situations from multiple sides or perspectives simultaneously

Stereoskopia was discovered on May 28, 1905, by Paul Götz and measures 168.16 km in diameter (although another measurement gives approximately 84 km). Stereoskopia owes its name to a photographic technique of overlapping double images that produce a stereoscopic or 3D effect. Remarkably in the discovery chart, the Sun conjunct Huya (karmic layers) is in Gemini; opposite Stereoskopia and square the North Node-South Node axis. In the natal chart, Stereoskopia seems to refer to the ability to perceive or consider something from various angles, perspectives, or viewpoints simultaneously, or in a negative sense, lose one's way due to too many perspectives, leading to a farce or a state of doubt. Forensically, the asteroid refers to everything related to 3D techniques.

The orbital period is 6 years and 82 days.

87 SYLVIA

Issues related to being buried alive (especially symbolically); extreme experiences in love or with life partners; forest

Sylvia was discovered on May 16, 1866, by Norman Robert Pogson. It is a dark, highly porous object, the 8th largest asteroid in the main belt, measuring 384×262×232 km. Sylvia is named after Rhea Sylvia and has two small moons: Romulus and Remus. Rhea Silvia, also known as Ilia, was the mythical mother of the twins Romulus and Remus, who were said to have founded the city of Rome. Her story is told in Livy's Ab Urbe Condita. According to Livy, she was the daughter of Numitor, king of Alba Longa, and a descendant of Aeneas. Numitor's younger brother Amulius seized the throne, killed Numitor's son, and then forced Rhea Silvia to become a Vestal Virgin, a priestess of the goddess Vesta. Like all Vestal Virgins, she had to swear a celibacy of thirty years, which would ensure that Numitor's line would have no heirs. However, Rhea Silvia became pregnant and gave birth to the twins Romulus and Remus. She claimed that the god Mars was the father of her children. Livy writes that she was raped by an unknown man but declared that Mars was the father of her children, either because she truly believed it or because it was less severe to have 'committed' such a crime with a god. When Amulius heard this, he ordered Rhea Silvia to be buried alive and instructed a servant to kill the twins. However, the servant couldn't bring himself to kill the twins and set them adrift on the Tiber River. The river carried the basket with the babies to a sandbank. A she-wolf (Lupa), who had just lost her own cubs, took them in and nursed the twins until Faustulus rescued the boys and raised them with his wife Larentia. Tiberinus, the god of the Tiber, then saved Rhea Silvia and married her. Romulus and Remus later headed to Rome, overthrew the rule of Amulius, and made Numitor king of Alba Longa again.

The name Rhea Silvia suggests a minor deity, a demigoddess of the forests. Silva means forest, and Rhea can be related to res and regnum; Rhea can also be related to the Greek rheo, flow, and therefore be related to her association with the god of the Tiber River or the Greek goddess Rhea. In the natal chart, Sylvia may refer to someone named Sylvia; to experiencing the sign or house where Sylvia is placed, or at least aspects of it, as a grave where one feels buried alive or, conversely, does everything to escape; to the fear of being buried alive or suffocated, to oppression; to a center of extreme experiences in love or relationship with the life partner; to a place where one feels rejected and deprived of self-expression; an emotionally heavy phase that one must endure for a greater good that will occur later. In the discovery chart, the Sun conjunct Algol and the very problematic Venus/Moon conjunction with the Centaurs Asbolus/2002 PN34/2001 SQ73 immediately stand out; trine the underworld-Plutino Mors-Somnus and trine Rhadamanthus. Sylvia can ultimately serve as a stepping stone to money, fame, and/or power at some point. In forensic astrology, Sylvia indicates a forest, people with the name Sylvia, or a location where someone is buried.

The orbital period is 6 years and 185 days.

466 TISIPHONE
Convictions; revenge; executions; false flag attacks and networks; satellite espionage; state lies

Tisiphone was discovered on January 17, 1901, by Max Wolf and Luigi Carnera and measures 115.53 km in diameter. The asteroid is named after the Greek goddess of revenge. Very harsh judgments or convictions; harsh legal proceedings; executions; death sentences; being tried for murder; shocking photographic evidence; sudden turns in forensic or scientific research; state lies and structural disinformation; espionage technology, satellite espionage, detection systems for long-distance observation; false flag attacks and networks; revenge that spoils one's own happiness.

The orbital period is 6 years and 58 days.

Thesiphone regem, reginamq3 in furorem agit.

909 ULLA

Persisting in a pattern or work routine until something compels a different perspective; honest acceptance and acknowledgment of a new truth and direction; empowerment of change; carbohydrate-rich diet; sexual drive; reigning or exercising power from the shadows

Ulla was discovered on February 17, 1919, by Karl Wilhelm Reinmuth and measures 116.44 km in diameter. Ulla was named after the daughter of a friend of the discoverer. The asteroid has a rather heavy earthly energy, somewhat Saturn-Pluto-like. Ulla makes one persistent in a pattern or work routine until something forces a different perspective. With a dominant Ulla, one does not like change, but every now and then has to deal with it, after which one consciously accepts and recognizes a new course or insight and integrates it. Ulla then becomes suitable for empowering that change or that new idea or insight. Ulla may seem inconsistent or arbitrary but is precisely not. A strong Ulla will often make someone adopt a vision or attitude during their life that radically opposes their former 'default setting', still colored by upbringing, personal history, culture, class, media indoctrination, or schooling. A new belief is passionately advocated when the overall horoscope points in that direction, but there is a risk of discarding valuable aspects by being excessively undiplomatic and overbearing. Ulla also shows a preference for a carbohydrate-rich diet and makes one sexually more active, capricious, and needy; the sex drive is very strong and can derail into addiction to pornography, masturbation, or other sex-related activities or obsessions. In a negative sense, Ulla has a link to ruling or exercising power from the shadows. Forensically, it can also refer to these themes.

The orbital period is 6 years and 243 days.

HELPFUL TIPS

When working with asteroids in addition to the traditional planets and sensitive points and angles, I recommend the use of very small aspect-orbs. In most cases a transit that makes a conjunction or opposition will only be felt between ½° before the minute exact aspect and ½° after. The strongest influence is felt during what we should name the "anaretic arcminutes". Thus at ½° before the minute exact conjunction, during the minute exact conjunction and at ½° (this rule includes even Sedna-Sun conjunctions). Plutinos are an exception as their transits are often already strong at one degree before the aspect is minute exact and dependent on their nature and size, there are also exceptions among objects of other asteroid classes.

You cannot investigate asteroids without either astro-software that includes them or proper online tools. The most useful websites are these:

serennu.com
Number 1 site for your personal asteroid astrology research. I would not have been able to produce this book and my other work on the subject without this superb initiative.

astro.com
I use the "extended chart option" of astro.com in assistance to serennu.com.

astro.com/swisseph/astlist.htm
Complete list of named asteroids.

http://www.true-node.com/eph3/
Very useful for creating an ephemeris.

ssd.jpl.nasa.gov/sbdb.cgi
NASA Jet Propulsion Laboratory asteroid-database.

minorplanetcenter.net/db_search/
Minor Planet Center asteroid-database.

minorplanetcenter.net/iau/lists/NumberedMPs.html
The MPC numbers and discovery dates of all known asteroids so far. If the asteroids received an official name you will find it there. The list starts with number 1: Ceres.
Recommended pioneering asteroid astrology sites:

zanestein.com/Trans-pluto.htm
Zane Stein is one of the most interesting pioneers in asteroid astrology of Centaurs and TNO's.

http://markandrewholmes.com/asteroid.html
Holmes provides a regularly updated list of both main-belt asteroids and other objects including Centaurs, SDOs, Plutinos and Cubewanos.

transneptunian-astrology.blogspot.com
This blog specializes in TNO's and Centaurs, with regular updates.

philipsedgwick.com
Interesting info on TNO's, dwarf planets, Centaurs and more.

vamzzz.com/blog/category/astrology
My own blog-section that deals with astrology, with regular updates.

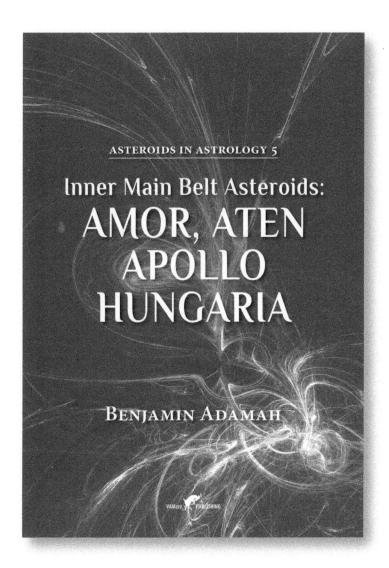

COMING SOON:
Amor, Aten, Apollo, Hungaria
Asteroids in Astrology 5

PAPER BOOKS

VAMzzz Publishing is a company that preserves historical occult books and produces new and revised editions in various categories such as Magic & Witchcraft, Secret Rites & Societies, Demonology, Celtic & Mythology, and New Astrology.

Our books are written by highly qualified academic researchers or experts in specific fields of esoteric knowledge, craft, or practice. Many of the revised titles include a Post Scriptum with additional information about the author or subject.

Our reproductions of classic texts differ from others in two important ways. Firstly, we have chosen not to rely on OCR (Optical Character Recognition) technology, as we believe that this often results in poor quality books that are littered with typos and other errors. Secondly, in cases where the original text contains images, such as portraits, maps, or sketches, we have taken great care to preserve the quality of these illustrations, ensuring that they accurately reflect the original artefact. By preserving and sharing these works, we can gain a deeper understanding of our cultural heritage and the rich history of human thought and creativity that has come before us.

VAMzzz Publishing
P.O. Box 3340
1001 AC Amsterdam
The Netherlands
vamzzz@protonmail.com
www.vamzzz.com

In addition to publishing books, VAMzzz Publishing also offers FREE articles on various occult topics, including Afro-American magic, folklore, and New Astrology on our blog. You are welcome to visit vamzzz.com/blog and explore these subjects further.

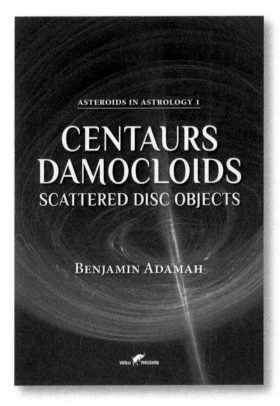

**Centaurs, Damocloids &
Scattered Disc Objects**
Asteroids in Astrology 1
162 pages • Hardcover
ISBN 9789492355409

Challenging the astrological status
quo, this book discusses the fascinating
astrological significance of no less
than 85 Centaurs and Centaur related
asteroids like Scattered Disc Objects
(SDOs) & Detached Objects, Damocloids,
retrograde Asteroids and (ex-) Comets.
Astronomy positions these unstable
objects with their unusual orbits at
the forefront of the evolutionary shifts in our Solar System. Analogue with this astronomical status,
the astrological newcomers described in this book are vital for a true understanding of out-of-
the-box thinking people, as well as complex Zeitgeist-issues and actual mundane phenomena.

Centaurs are of major psychological importance, and as is the case with the first discovered Centaur
Chiron, most of them are about healing and psycho-synthesis. Thus they intrinsically deal with the
converging of opposed, often extreme characteristics into a flow of productive synergy and creative
power. See Nessus, Pylenor, Pholus, Hylonome, Bienor, Crantor, Thereus, Asbolus, to mention but a
few. We have already used the now "standardized" Chiron (218 km in diameter) for years, but why
are many much bigger objects like SDO / dwarf planet Eris (diameter of 2326 km) still ignored?

See Eris' role in great demonstrations and (with Typhon) in major disasters like Fukushima. Can we
truly understand the disintegration of the former USSR while skipping Damocles, the NSA without
2002 RP120, or Edward Snowden without Kondojiro? Not including SDOs like Eris and 1999 TD10 in
(geo)political astrology is an almost provocative way of jumping to false conclusions. 2000 CO104,
2007 TG422 and 2005 PQ21 shed their (taboo breaking) lights on orgasm and sex, while you'll
be amazed at the application of 1998 BU48, 1996 TL66 and 2001 BL41 in financial astrology...

Plutinos
Asteroids in Astrology 2
126 pages • Hardcover
ISBN 9789492355522

Plutinos are asteroids and in some cases dwarf planet candidates, circling around in the inner Kuiper belt, in orbits comparable to the one of Pluto (Pluto-Charon). Astrological research points out that most Plutinos, like their godfather Pluto, exert a compelling force in both personal and mundane horoscopes. They are radical, transforming, confronting, they penetrate the darkness, the blur, or daily life patterns and have a Scorpio-like preference for what you might call soul-mining. They trigger the awareness of slumbering patterns in the depths of our souls and force us to face the truth.

Most Plutinos are "isolating" one or two classic Plutonian keywords, such as: intensifying, dark, transforming, cutting away dead wood, letting go, death, discharging, imploding, violence, criminality, rebellion, dirt, sex, penetration, psychopaths or the occult. Strong transits, to or from these slow moving asteroids, can act as serious turning points in our lives. Negatively, several Plutinos exacerbate those qualities belonging to the darker side of Pluto and its sign Scorpio. All members of this classification fill in many gaps in chart interpretations, adding much to both personal and mundane astrology.

After his 2019 debut on Centaurs, Damocloids and SDO's, Benjamin Adamah now presents the astrological meaning of 44 Plutinos. Apart from Orcus(-Vanth), Ixion, Arawn, Huya, Lempo(-Hiisi), Mors-Somnus and Rhadamantus, 37 other important Plutinos, cataloged by MPC-number, are discussed. This book comes with a special appendix about the chart of the USA and its crucial role within the current world-crisis. This analysis is based on Plutinos and the Black Sun-Diamond axis. A second appendix shows a substantial list of Pluto-Charon aspects with asteroids of several classes which – like the Plutinos – have specific Plutonic features in common with the gatekeeper of our solar system.

Cubewanos, Haumeids & other TNOs
Asteroids in Astrology 3
110 pages • Hardcover
ISBN 9789492355645

The Cubewanos get more and more attention in astrology. They form a group of asteroids and dwarf-planets in the Kuiper Belt, just beyond the orbit of Pluto. Their orbital period around the Sun is 260 to 330 years. To be classified as a Cubewano, the asteroid must be quite large (at least about 100 km in diameter).

Cubewanos are complex objects, but mainly because of their versatility and less because of inherent conflicts or wounds as with Centaurs and Jupiter Trojans, or obsessive tendencies as seen with Plutinos. Many of these objects are connected to Zeitgeist-phenomena that characterize the 21st century. For example, Quaoar governs growth and expansion through wiki-like structures. Makemake governs new technology, microbiology, satellites, skyscrapers, peak performance, and experiences in all possible fields. Varuna is about major massmedia-events, Many Cubewanos already attracted the attention of astrologers, like Albion (QB1), Logos, Varda, Praamzius, Chaos, Arroboth, Altjirah, Sila-Nunam, Salacia, Borasisi, Deucalion and Teharonhiawako, while this book also covers many interesting Cubewanos that have not been officially named yet. The Haumeids are a group of asteroids that are all connected to the "mother object" Haumea. These fascinating objects are primarily about (distorted) dept-psychological dramas. Additionally, several Trans-Neptunian Objects are discussed with deviant orbits, including Manwë.

In this third publication of the asteroid-series, Benjamin Adamah explores the astrological significance of 29 Cubewanos, 10 Haumeids, and 11 TNOs with deviant Neptune resonances. Discover the influence of these celestial bodies in worldly affairs and how they impact your personal life!

Spirit Beings in European Folklore 1

292 descriptions – Ireland, England, Wales, Cornwall, Scotland, Isle of Man, Orkney's, Hebrides, Faeroe, Iceland, Norway, Sweden and Denmark
250 pages • Paperback • ISBN 9789492355553

Compendium 1 of the Spirit Beings in European Folklore-series covers the northwestern part of the continent where Celtic and Anglo-Saxon cultures meet the Nordic. This book catalogs the mysterious creatures of Ireland, the Isle of Man, England, Wales, Cornwall, Scotland, Hebrides, Orkneys, Faroe Islands, Iceland, Norway, Sweden and Denmark. For centuries, the peoples of these regions have influenced each other in many ways, including their mythologies and folklore. The latter is perhaps most evident in the various species of Brook-horses or Water-horses. These semi-aquatic ghostly creatures come in all kinds of varieties and are typical of the English or Gaelic speaking parts of Europe and Scandinavia. Many other ghostly entities occur only in specific areas or countries. Some even became cultural icons, such as the Irish Leprechaun, the Knockers from Wales, the Scandinavian Trolls and Huldras or the Icelandic Huldufólk. England has its Brownies, several kinds of Fairies and locally famous ghost dogs. Iceland and Scandinavia seem to "specialize" in spirit beings who appear fully materialized, such as the different species of Illveli (Evil Whales) and Draugr, the returning dead.

Spirit Beings in European Folklore 2

228 descriptions – Germany, Austria, Alpine regions, Switzerland, Netherlands, Flanders, Luxembourg, Lithuania, Latvia, Estonia, Finland, Jewish influences
256 pages • Paperback • ISBN 9789492355560

Compendium 2 of the Spirit Beings in European Folklore-series covers the German-speaking parts of Central Europe, the Low Countries, the Baltic region and Finland. Via the Ashkenazi Jews, spirit beings from the Middle East entered Central European culture, which are also included. This originally densely forested part of the continent is particularly rich in nature-spirits and has a wide variety of beings that dwell in forests and mountainous areas (Berggeister) or act as atmospheric forces. Also dominant are the many field-spirits and variations of Alp-like creatures (Mare, Nightmare). There is an overlap with the Nordic and Eastern European Revenant and Vampire-types, and we find several water- and sea-spirits. Among the German-speaking and Baltic peoples, invoking field-spirits was an integrated part of agriculture, with rites continuing into the early 20th century. The Alpine regions have spirits who watch over cattle. In general, forest-spirits are prominent. Germany has its Moosweiblein and Wilder Mann (Woodwose), the Baltic region has its Mātes, and Finland its Metsän Väki. Then there are ghostly animals, and earth- and house-spirits such as the many kinds of Kobolds, the Dutch Kabouter, and the Kaukas of Prussia and Latvia.

Spirit Beings in European Folklore 3

255 descriptions – Russia, Belarus, Ukraine, Poland, Romania, Hungary, Bulgaria, Czechia, Slovenia, Serbia, Croatia, Albania, Georgia, Turkish regions, Roma-culture
246 pages • Paperback • ISBN 9789492355577

Compendium 3 of the Spirit Beings in European Folklore-series offers an overview of the mysterious, sometimes beautiful and often shadowy entities of the Slavic countries, the Balkans, the Carpathians, Albania, Georgia, and the Turkish and Romani peoples. Many types of Vampires and vampiric Revenants are included – in their original state and purged of later applied disinformation. The undead are prominent in the folklore of Eastern Europe and Albania. Also typical are farm- and household-spirits such as the Domovoy, water-spirits and forest demons like the Russian Leshy, the Chuhaister, or the evil Polish Bełt, who like the Ukrainian Blud, leads travelers off their path until they are lost in the deepest part of the forest. Unique is the Russian Bannik or spirit of the bathhouse. Amongst the Slavs, some 'demons', like the Boginka for example, originally belonged to the pre-Christian pantheon. Eastern Europe, in contrast to its returning dead, is rich in seductive female spirits such as the Romanian Iele, the Russian Russalka, the Vila of the Eastern and Southern Slavs and the Bulgarian Samodiva. Via the Balkans, Greek influences entered Slavic culture, while there are also spirits that intersect Germanic and Nordic folklore.

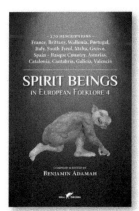

Spirit Beings in European Folklore 4

270 descriptions – France, Brittany, Wallonia, Portugal, Italy, South Tyrol, Malta, Greece, Spain – Basque Country, Asturias, Catalonia, Cantabria, Galicia, Valencia
250 pages • Paperback • ISBN 9789492355584

Compendium 4 of the Spirit Beings in European Folklore-series covers an area that starts with Wallonia and continues via France and the Pyrenees, through the Iberian Peninsula, to Italy and Greece. This results in a very diverse and colourful collection of spirit beings, due to the many included Basque nature-spirits or Ireluak, the Spanish Duendes, the Celtic spirits of Brittany, the prankster Italian Folletti and the creatures from Greece. Some creatures from Breton folklore are particularly gruesome, such as the hollow-eyed Ankou, the Werewolf-like Bugul-nôz, or the ghostly and Will-o'-the-wisp-like Yan-gant-y-tan, who roams the night roads with his five lit candles. Most Italian ghosts are less gloomy, while the Iberian Peninsula is home to everything ranging from the 'Beauty' to the 'Beast'. Compendium 4 contains – amongst other things – many kinds of dwarf-spirits or Goblins (Lutins, Nutons, Folletti, Farfadettes, Korrigans, Minairons) various seductive and feminine spring creatures, Wild Man-varieties (Basajaunak, Jentilak) and an extensive section on the Incubus-Succubus. It is fascinating to discover how many types of European spirit beings (from Kobold to many female spring-spirits), described in the other Compendiums, can be traced back to creatures from Ancient Greece.

www.ingramcontent.com/pod-product-compliance
Lightning Source LLC
LaVergne TN
LVHW071454140725
816105LV00011B/152